# The Wade
# Collectors Handbook
# and Price Guide

### Stella Ashbrook

*Francis Joseph*
ISBN 1-870703-19-7

# Acknowledgements

Wade is a vast and interesting subject and having sold Wade for many years through auction, (and having compiled sections of this book), I feel I have gleamed an insight to why it is so collectable. Prices have been fluctuating on the secondary market over the past few years, but as with any collectable there are high and low spots. As a collectable it is timeless, as many generations remember seeing a piece of Wade that reminds them of their childhood.

My thanks go to Kris Butler who gave up his valuable time to enable us to photograph his collection as well as helping with information and values included in this edition. Trevor Leek for the photography and Frank Salmon the Publisher for his unreserved time and effort in the production of this book, and the experienced assistance of John Folkard, which has been much appreciated.

Collectors have been inspiring and my family a huge support, I thank them all.

The Wade Price Guide
© 2003 Francis Joseph Publications
2nd edition

Published in the UK by
Francis Joseph Publications
5 Southbrook Mews, London SE12 8LG
Telephone: 020 8318 9580

Typeset by E J Folkard Computer Services
199 Station Road, Crayford, Kent DA1 3QF

Printed by
Red Design and Print Ltd, England

ISBN 1-870703-19-7

# Contents

# Foreword

The novelty value of Wade still holds strong and with the fluctuating collecting markets it has weathered the test of time. The Whimsies that are the most recognisable as Wade first appeared in 1954 at the British Industries Fair, the inexpensive miniature animals attracted interest from all ages and still do today.

The huge attraction of the Whimsical models today makes the earlier models with original boxes very collectable. They don't appear on the secondary market regularly and when they do come up via auction or the Internet, there is a guaranteed international response. The initial years of Whimsical production haven't changed other than the more efficient methods of manufacturing, the characters that are still produced relate to famous Disney characters, novelty nursery rhyme figures, comic characters and famous people, all appealing and directed at the discerning collector.

The collectable market today is under enormous pressure to provide collectables that are affordable and can not only be purchased as an interest but have the added advantage of retaining its value on the secondary market as each year goes by. Wade has achieved remarkable secondary market prices over the past eight years, but as with all collectable markets, the buyers for the goods can change their direction overnight by just reading an article on a new product line or an old forgotten nostalgic newspaper clipping and before you know it collecting stamps is back in fashion!

Wade as a collectable is one of the most accessible and will appeal to all, so if you have a young collector in the family who wants to enjoy the chase of finding the elusive pieces, initially it won't break the bank. However, when the interest takes on that inevitable addiction to Wade Fairs, Antique Fairs, Carboots, Auctions and trawling the Internet, its advisable they get a Saturday job or increase their allowance!!

Good luck to all old and new collectors – happy hunting.

# Whimsies

## ENGLISH ANIMALS
### Set 1 – 1954-1958

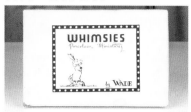 

155

| Item | Description | Size (mm) | Market Value | | Acquired |
|------|-------------|-----------|--------------|--|----------|
| Leaping Fawn | White/Green base | 40x40 | £20-£30 | $30-$45 | ☐ |
| Horse | Brown/Green/Brown base | 35x50 | £20-£30 | $30-$45 | ☐ |
| Spaniel with ball | White/Grey | 25x40 | £20-£30 | $30-$45 | ☐ |
| Poodle | Brown/White | 35x35 | £25-£35 | $35-$55 | ☐ |
| Squirrel | Light Grey | 25x50 | £20-£30 | $30-$45 | ☐ |

## ENGLISH ANIMALS
### Set 2 – 1954-1958

250

| Item | Description | Size (mm) | Market Value | | Acquired |
|------|-------------|-----------|--------------|--|----------|
| Bull | Brown/Green base | 45x55 | £50-£70 | $75-$105 | ☐ |
| Lamb | Brown/Green base | 45x25 | £25-£30 | $35-$45 | ☐ |
| Kitten | White/Grey/Blue base | 15x40 | £40-£60 | $60-$90 | ☐ |
| Hare | Grey/White base | 30x40 | £20-£30 | $30-$45 | ☐ |
| Dachshund | Beige | 35x45 | £40-£60 | $60-$90 | ☐ |

## ENGLISH COUNTRY ANIMALS
### Set 3 – 1955-1958

190

| Item | Description | Size (mm) | Market Value | | Acquired |
|------|-------------|-----------|--------------|--|----------|
| Badger | Grey/Black | 30x40 | £20-£30 | $30-$45 | ☐ |
| Fox Cub | Light Brown | 35x35 | £30-£50 | $45-$75 | ☐ |
| Stoat | Grey tail/Red eyes | 20x35 | £30-£50 | $45-$75 | ☐ |
| Shetland Pony | Grey mane/Green base | 35x40 | £20-£30 | $30-$45 | ☐ |
| Retriever | Brown, Green/White base | 30x40 | £20-£30 | $30-$45 | ☐ |

# AFRICAN JUNGLE ANIMALS
## Set 4 – 1955-1958

185

| Item | Description | Size (mm) | Market Value | | Acquired |
|------|-------------|-----------|--------------|--|----------|
| Lion | Light Brown | 30x35 | £30-£40 | $45-$60 | ☐ |
| Crocodile | Green/Brown | 15x40 | £35-£45 | $50-$70 | ☐ |
| Monkey & Baby | Brown | 45x25 | £20-£30 | $30-$45 | ☐ |
| Rhinoceros | Grey | 45x45 | £20-£30 | $30-$45 | ☐ |
| Baby Elephant | Grey | 40x40 | £30-£40 | $45-$60 | ☐ |

# HORSES
## Set 5 – 1956-1959

| Item | Description | Size (mm) | Market Value | | Acquired |
|------|-------------|-----------|--------------|--|----------|
| Mare | White/Brown mane/Green base | 45x40 | £30-£40 | $45-$60 | ☐ |
| Mare | Light Brown, Green base | 45x40 | £30-£40 | $45-$60 | ☐ |
| Foal | Light Brown, Green base | 40x40 | £30-£40 | $45-$60 | ☐ |
| Foal | Dark Brown, Green base | 40x40 | £30-£40 | $45-$60 | ☐ |
| Foal | White, Brown mane, Green base | 45x40 | £30-£40 | $45-$60 | ☐ |
| Colt | Light Brown, Green base | 40x40 | £30-£40 | $45-$60 | ☐ |
| Beagle | Brown patches, Green base | 20x20 | £35-£45 | $50-$70 | ☐ |

285

# POLAR ANIMALS
## Set 6 – 1956-1959

| Item | Description | Size (mm) | Market Value | | Acquired |
|------|-------------|-----------|--------------|---|----------|
| King Penquin | Yellow beak & feet | 35x20 | £30-£50 | $45-$75 | ☐ |
| Husky | Fawn/Grey | 30x25 | £30-£50 | $45-$75 | ☐ |
| Polar Bear | Blue base | 45x45 | £25-£30 | $35-$45 | ☐ |
| Baby Seal | Grey/White base | 25x25 | £20-£30 | $30-$45 | ☐ |
| Polar Bear Cub | White | 20x30 | £25-£30 | $35-$45 | ☐ |
| Polar Bear Cub | Pink | 20x30 | £25-£30 | $35-$45 | ☐ |

# PEDIGREE DOGS
## Set 7 – 1957-1961

| Item | Description | Size (mm) | Market Value | | Acquired |
|------|-------------|-----------|--------------|---|----------|
| Alsation | Grey/Brown | 35x40 | £20-£30 | $30-$45 | ☐ |
| West Highland Terrier | White | 25x35 | £25-£30 | $35-$45 | ☐ |
| Corgi | Beige/White | 25x30 | £25-£30 | $35-$45 | ☐ |
| Boxer | Brown | 35x40 | £25-£30 | $35-$45 | ☐ |
| St Bernard | Brown/White | 40x45 | £30-£40 | $45-$60 | ☐ |

# ZOO ANIMALS
## Set 8 – 1957-1961

*The Large Giant Panda is often mistakenly thought part of this set. It is shown here for comparison purposes.*

| Item | Description | Size (mm) | Market Value | | Acquired |
|------|-------------|-----------|--------------|---|----------|
| Llama | Grey face, Brown/Green base | 45x30 | £20-£30 | $30-$45 | ☐ |
| Lion Cub | Brown & White | 25x25 | £20-£30 | $30-$45 | ☐ |
| Giant Panda, small | Black/White, Black band on chest | 30x18 | £20-£30 | $30-$45 | ☐ |
| Giant Panda, large | Black/White | 35x25 | £20-£30 | $30-$45 | ☐ |
| Bactrian Camel | Light Brown, Green base | 40x40 | £25-£30 | $35-$45 | ☐ |
| Cockatoo | Yellow crest, Grey base | 30x30 | £25-£30 | $35-$45 | ☐ |

# NORTH AMERICAN ANIMALS
## Set 9 – 1958-1961

| Item | Description | Size (mm) | Market Value | | Acquired |
|------|-------------|-----------|--------------|---|----------|
| Snowy Owl | Brown eyes | 28x30 | £30-£40 | $45-$60 | ☐ |
| Racoon | Grey/Black | 30x30 | £20-£30 | $30-$45 | ☐ |
| Grizzly Bear | Brown/White | 50x25 | £30-£40 | $45-$60 | ☐ |
| Grizzly Cub | Light Brown | 25x25 | £20-£30 | $30-$45 | ☐ |
| Grizzly Cub | Brown | 25x30 | £20-£30 | $30-$45 | ☐ |
| Grizzly Cub | White | 25x25 | £30-£40 | $45-$60 | ☐ |
| Cougar | Brown/White | 20x45 | £30-£40 | $45-$60 | ☐ |

# FARM ANIMALS
## Set 10 – 1959-1961

| Item | Description | Size (mm) | Market Value | | Acquired |
|------|-------------|-----------|--------------|---|----------|
| Pig | Pink | 20x35 | £40-£60 | $60-$90 | ☐ |
| Italian Goat | Grey | 30x30 | £40-£60 | $60-$90 | ☐ |
| Italian Goat | Beige | 30x30 | £60-£80 | $90-$120 | ☐ |
| Foxhound | Beige/Green base | 25x45 | £40-£60 | $60-$90 | ☐ |
| Foxhound | Brown Green/White base | 25x45 | £40-£60 | $60-$90 | ☐ |
| Shire Horse | Creamy beige RARE | 50x50 | £130-£150 | $190-$230 | ☐ |
| Shire Horse | White | 50x40 | £120-£140 | $180-$215 | ☐ |
| Shire Horse | Red Brown VERY RARE | 50x50 | £130-£180 | $190-$275 | ☐ |
| Swan | Yellow beak | 25x35 | £100-£120 | $150-$185 | ☐ |

# WHIMSIES DOGS AND PUPPIES – 1969-1982

### Set 1 – Alsatian – 1969-1982

| Item | Description | Size (mm) | Market Value | | Acquired |
|------|-------------|-----------|--------------|---|----------|
| Mother | Brown | 60x75 | £12-£20 | $20-$30 | ☐ |
| Puppy Sitting | Brown | 40x45 | £8-£12 | $10-$20 | ☐ |
| Puppy Lying | Brown | 35x45 | £8-£12 | $10-$20 | ☐ |

*24*

### Set 2 – Cairn – 1969-1982

| Item | Description | Size (mm) | Market Value | | Acquired |
|------|-------------|-----------|--------------|---|----------|
| Mother | Honey Brown | 65x70 | £12-£20 | $20-$30 | ☐ |
| Puppy Standing | Honey Brown | 40x50 | £8-£12 | $10-$20 | ☐ |
| Puppy Lying | Honey Brown | 35x50 | £8-£12 | $10-$20 | ☐ |

### Set 3 – Red Setter – 1973-1982

*44*

| Item | Description | Size (mm) | Market Value | | Acquired |
|------|-------------|-----------|--------------|---|----------|
| Mother | Red/Brown | 60x75 | £10-£20 | $15-$30 | ☐ |
| Puppy Lying, Right | Red/Brown | 40x45 | £10-£20 | $15-$30 | ☐ |
| Puppy Lying Left | Red/Brown | 40x45 | £10-£20 | $15-$30 | ☐ |

*60*

### Set 4 – Corgi – 1979-1982

| Item | Description | Size (mm) | Market Value | | Acquired |
|------|-------------|-----------|--------------|---|----------|
| Mother | Honey Brown | 60x60 | £30-£40 | $45-$60 | ☐ |
| Puppy Sitting | Honey Brown | 45x40 | £20-£25 | $30-$40 | ☐ |
| Puppy lying | Honey Brown | 30x45 | £20-£25 | $30-$40 | ☐ |

*40*

### Set 5 – Yorkshire Terrier – 1979-1982

| Item | Description | Size (mm) | Market Value | | Acquired |
|------|-------------|-----------|--------------|---|----------|
| Mother | Black/Brown | 55x70 | £30-£40 | $45-$60 | ☐ |
| Puppy Sitting | Black/Brown | 40x40 | £30-£40 | $45-$60 | ☐ |
| Puppy Walking | Black/Brown | 35x45 | £30-£40 | $45-$60 | ☐ |

*80*

# ENGLISH WHIMSIES: 1971-1984

**Set 1: Blue box – 1971**

| Item | Description | Size (mm) | Market Value | | Acquired |
|------|-------------|-----------|-------------|---|----------|
| Fawn | Brown | 30x30 | £4-£12 | $5-$20 | ☐ |
| Rabbit | Beige | 30x30 | £4-£12 | $5-$20 | ☐ |
| Mongrel | Dark Brown | 35x35 | £4-£12 | $5-$20 | ☐ |
| Kitten | Pink wool | 30x30 | £4-£12 | $5-$20 | ☐ |
| Kitten | Red wool | 30x30 | £4-£8 | $5-$10 | ☐ |
| Spaniel | Honey | 35x35 | £4-£8 | $5-$10 | ☐ |

**Set 2: Red box –1972**

6 1

| Item | Description | Size (mm) | Market Value | | Acquired |
|------|-------------|-----------|-------------|---|----------|
| Duck | Blue/Brown | 30x40 | £4-£8 | $5-$10 | ☐ |
| Corgi | Honey | 30x35 | £4-£8 | $5-$10 | ☐ |
| Beaver | Grey/Brown | 35x45 | £4-£8 | $5-$10 | ☐ |
| Bushbaby | Brown | 30x30 | £4-£8 | $5-$10 | ☐ |
| Fox | Dark Brown | 30x30 | £4-£8 | $5-$10 | ☐ |

**Set 3: Dark Green box – 1972**

40

| Item | Description | Size (mm) | Market Value | | Acquired |
|------|-------------|-----------|-------------|---|----------|
| Setter | Brown | 35x50 | £4-£8 | $5-$10 | ☐ |
| Owl | Dark Brown | 35x20 | £4-£8 | $5-$10 | ☐ |
| Otter | Beige | 30x35 | £4-£8 | $5-$10 | ☐ |
| Trout | Brown | 30x30 | £4-£8 | $5-$10 | ☐ |
| Bear cub | Grey | 30x40 | £4-£8 | $5-$10 | ☐ |

40

**Set 4: Yellow box – 1973**

| Item | Description | Size (mm) | Market Value | | Acquired |
|---|---|---|---|---|---|
| Chimpanzee | Dark Brown | 35x35 | £4-£8 | $5-$10 | ☐ |
| Hippo | Large Honey | 25x45 | £10-£15 | $15-$25 | ☐ |
| Hippo | Small Honey | 20x40 | £4-£8 | $5-$10 | ☐ |
| Lion | Light Brown | 35x45 | £4-£8 | $5-$10 | ☐ |
| Elephant | Grey | 35x28 | £8-£12 | $10-$20 | ☐ |
| Giraffe | Beige | 35x35 | £4-£8 | $5-$10 | ☐ |

**Set 5: Dark Red box – 1974**

*59*

| Item | Description | Size (mm) | Market Value | | Acquired |
|---|---|---|---|---|---|
| Alsatian | Grey | 30x40 | £4-£8 | $5-$10 | ☐ |
| Field Mouse | Yellow/Brown | 35x25 | £4-£8 | $5-$10 | ☐ |
| Pine Martin | Honey | 30x30 | £4-£8 | $5-$10 | ☐ |
| Hedgehog | Dark Brown | 25x40 | £4-£8 | $5-$10 | ☐ |
| Squirrel | Grey | 35x30 | £4-£8 | $5-$10 | ☐ |

**Set 6: Light Blue box – 1975**

*40*

| Item | Description | Size (mm) | Market Value | | Acquired |
|---|---|---|---|---|---|
| Collie | Brown | 35x35 | £5-£8 | $8-$10 | ☐ |
| Cow | Honey | 35x35 | £5-£8 | $8-$10 | ☐ |
| Pig | Large/beige | 27x44 | £12-£18 | $20-$30 | ☐ |
| Pig | Med/beige | 25x40 | £10-£12 | $15-$20 | ☐ |
| Pig | Small/beige | 25x35 | £10-£12 | $15-$20 | ☐ |
| Horse | Dark Grey | 35x35 | £5-£8 | $8-$10 | ☐ |
| Lamb | Brown | 30x25 | £5-£8 | $8-$10 | ☐ |

*74*

## Set 7: Orange box – 1976

| Item | Description | Size (mm) | Market Value | | Acquired |
|------|-------------|-----------|--------------|--|----------|
| Camel | Light Brown | 35x35 | £5-£8 | $8-$10 | ☐ |
| Zebra | Black | 40x35 | £30-£40 | $45-$60 | ☐ |
| Zebra | Light Brown | 40x35 | £5-£8 | $8-$10 | ☐ |
| Leopard | Yellow | 17x45 | £5-£8 | $8-$10 | ☐ |
| Rhino | Grey | 25x35 | £5-£8 | $8-$10 | ☐ |
| Gorilla | Grey | 35x25 | £5-£8 | $8-$10 | ☐ |

## Set 8: Magenta box – 1977

| Item | Description | Size (mm) | Market Value | | Acquired |
|------|-------------|-----------|--------------|--|----------|
| Donkey | Light Brown | 30x30 | £8-£12 | $10-$20 | ☐ |
| Barn Owl | Light Brown | 35x20 | £8-£12 | $10-$20 | ☐ |
| Cat | Light Brown | 40x17 | £8-£12 | $10-$20 | ☐ |
| Mouse | Beige | 40x25 | £8-£12 | $10-$20 | ☐ |
| Ram | White | 30x30 | £6-£10 | $8-$15 | ☐ |

## Set 9: Blue box – 1978

| Item | Description | Size (mm) | Market Value | | Acquired |
|------|-------------|-----------|--------------|--|----------|
| Dolphin | Grey | 30x40 | £20-£25 | $30-$40 | ☐ |
| Pelican | Brown | 45x40 | £8-£12 | $10-$20 | ☐ |
| Angel Fish | Dark Grey | 35x30 | £6-£10 | $8-$15 | ☐ |
| Turtle | Grey/Green | 15x15 | £5-£8 | $8-$10 | ☐ |
| Seahorse | Yellow | 50x17 | £8-£12 | $10-$20 | ☐ |

12

## Set 10: Pale Green box – 1979

| Item | Description | Size (mm) | Market Value | | Acquired |
|------|-------------|-----------|--------------|---|----------|
| Kangaroo | Dark Brown | 45x25 | £6-£10 | $8-$15 | ☐ |
| Orang-Utan | Ginger | 30x30 | £5-£8 | $8-$10 | ☐ |
| Tiger | Yellow | 35x25 | £10-£12 | $15-$20 | ☐ |
| Koala Bear | Yellow/Brown | 35x25 | £15-£20· | $20-$30 | ☐ |
| Langur | Light Brown | 35x30 | £5-£8 | $8-$10 | ☐ |

## Set 11: Dark Brown box – 1979

*5 8*

| Item | Description | Size (mm) | Market Value | | Acquired |
|------|-------------|-----------|--------------|---|----------|
| Bison | Large, Honey | 32x45 | £5-£8 | $8-$10 | ☐ |
| Bison | Small, Honey | 28x40 | £5-£8 | $8-$10 | ☐ |
| Bluebird | Blue wings | 15x35 | £5-£8 | $8-$10 | ☐ |
| Bullfrog | Brown | 15x30 | £12-£18 | $20-$30 | ☐ |
| Wild Boar | Light Brown | 30x40 | £5-£8 | $8-$10 | ☐ |
| Raccoon | Brown | 25x35 | £8-£12 | $10-$20 | ☐ |

## Set 12: Dark Blue Box – 1980

*62*

| Item | Description | Size (mm) | Market Value | | Acquired |
|------|-------------|-----------|--------------|---|----------|
| Walrus | Light Brown | 30x30 | £5-£8 | $8-$10 | ☐ |
| Polar Bear | White | 30x30 | £12-£18 | $20-$30 | ☐ |
| Penquin | Grey | 38x19 | £15-£20 | $20-$30 | ☐ |
| Seal Pup | Beige | 25x37 | £8-£12 | $10-$20 | ☐ |
| Husky | Grey | 35x30 | £10-£15 | $15-$25 | ☐ |

*73*

# MINIKINS
## Cats: Series A – 1955-1958

| Item | Description | Size (mm) | Market Value | | Acquired |
|------|-------------|-----------|--------------|--|----------|
| Cat Walking | White, Blue ears | 20x38 | £12-£18 | $20-$30 | ☐ |
| Cat Walking | White, Yellow ears | 20x38 | £12-£18 | $20-$30 | ☐ |
| Cat Walking | White, Green eyes | 20x38 | £12-£18 | $20-$30 | ☐ |
| Cat Standing | Brown | 30x17 | £12-£18 | $20-$30 | ☐ |
| Cat Standing | White, Green ears | 30x17 | £12-£18 | $20-$30 | ☐ |
| Cat Standing | White, Green ears | 30x17 | £12-£18 | $20-$30 | ☐ |
| Cat Standing | White, Green eyes | 30x17 | £12-£18 | $20-$30 | ☐ |
| Cat Standing | White, Green starburst | 30x17 | £12-£18 | $20-$30 | ☐ |
| Cat Standing | White, Red starburst | 30x17 | £12-£18 | $20-$30 | ☐ |
| Cat Standing | White, Blue starburst | 30x17 | £12-£18 | $20-$30 | ☐ |
| Cat standing | White, Green daisy | 30x17 | £12-£18 | $20-$30 | ☐ |

## Rabbits: Series A – 1955-1958

| Item | Description | Size (mm) | Market Value | | Acquired |
|------|-------------|-----------|--------------|--|----------|
| Rabbit Sitting | Brown, Turquoise ears | 30x18 | £12-£18 | $20-$30 | ☐ |
| Rabbit Sitting | White, Blue ears | 30x18 | £12-£18 | $20-$30 | ☐ |
| Rabbit Sitting | White, Green ears, Blue patch, open eyes | 30x18 | £12-£18 | $20-$30 | ☐ |
| Rabbit Sitting | White, Green ears, Blue patch, winky eyes | 30x18 | £12-£18 | $20-$30 | ☐ |
| Rabbit Sitting | White, Yellow ears, open eyes | 30x18 | £12-£18 | $20-$30 | ☐ |
| Rabbit Sitting | White, Yellow ears, winky eyes | 30x18 | £12-£18 | $20-$30 | ☐ |
| Rabbit Sitting | White, Turquoise ears | 30x18 | £12-£18 | $20-$30 | ☐ |
| Narrow eared | White, Green ears, Blue patch | 30x18 | £12-£18 | $20-$30 | ☐ |
| Narrow eared | White, yellow ears, Blue patch | 30x18 | £12-£18 | $20-$30 | ☐ |
| Narrow eared | White, Black nose, Blue patch | 30x18 | £12-£18 | $20-$30 | ☐ |
| Narrow eared | White, Red nose, Blue OXO | 30x18 | £12-£18 | $20-$30 | ☐ |
| Narrow eared | White, Red nose, Green OXO | 30x18 | £12-£18 | $20-$30 | ☐ |
| Narrow eared | White, Red nose, Green/Red OXO | 30x18 | £12-£18 | $20-$30 | ☐ |

14

## Mouse: Series B – 1956-1958

| Item | Description | Size (mm) | Market Value | | Acquired |
|------|-------------|-----------|--------------|--|----------|
| Mouse | Brown | 25x23 | £12-£18 | $20-$30 | ☐ |
| Mouse | Brown, dark Blue patch | 25x23 | £12-£18 | $20-$30 | ☐ |
| Mouse | White all over | 25x23 | £12-£18 | $20-$30 | ☐ |
| Mouse | White, Blue patch | 25x23 | £12-£18 | $20-$30 | ☐ |
| Mouse | White, Green ears, Orange/ Green daisy | 25x23 | £12-£18 | $20-$30 | ☐ |
| Mouse | White, Green ears, Orange/ Green notes | 25x23 | £12-£18 | $20-$30 | ☐ |
| Mouse | White, Green ears, Red/ Green L plate | 25x23 | £12-£18 | $20-$30 | ☐ |
| Mouse | White, Pink ears, Blue/Red notes, Blue daisy | 25x23 | £12-£18 | $20-$30 | ☐ |
| Mouse | White, Pink ears, Blue heart/Green arrow, Blue daisy | 25x23 | £12-£18 | $20-$30 | ☐ |
| Mouse | White, Yellow ears, Blue/Green Red/ Blue notes | 25x23 | £12-£18 | $20-$30 | ☐ |
| Mouse | White, Yellow ears, Green daisy/ heart/Blue arrow | 25x23 | £12-£18 | $20-$30 | ☐ |
| Mouse | White, Yellow ears, Red/Orange L | 25x23 | £12-£18 | $20-$30 | ☐ |
| Mouse | White, Yellow ears, Orange daisy/ Orange/Blue notes | 25x23 | £12-£18 | $20-$30 | ☐ |

## Rabbit: Series B – 1956-1958

| Item | Description | Size (mm) | Market Value | | Acquired |
|------|-------------|-----------|--------------|--|----------|
| Wide eared | White, Red/Green flower, Red heart | 25x20 | £12-£18 | $20-$30 | ☐ |
| Wide eared | White, Green ears, Red heart/Green arrow, Blue heart/Green arrow | 25x20 | £12-£18 | $20-$30 | ☐ |
| Wide eared | White, Pink ears, Orange daisy/ Orange L | 25x20 | £12-£18 | $20-$30 | ☐ |
| Wide eared | White, Pink ears, Red L | 25x20 | £12-£18 | $20-$30 | ☐ |
| Wide eared | White, Yellow ears, Blue/Green notes/Blue/Green arrow | 25x20 | £12-£18 | $20-$30 | ☐ |
| Wide eared | White, Yellow ears, Red heart/ Blue arrow | 25x20 | £12-£18 | $20-$30 | ☐ |

## Bull: Series B – 1956-1958

| Item | Description | Size (mm) | Market Value | | Acquired |
|------|-------------|-----------|--------------|---|----------|
| Bull | Brown, Black spot | 20x25 | £12-£18 | $20-$30 | ☐ |
| Bull | Brown, Black spot/Yellow X | 20x25 | £12-£18 | $20-$30 | ☐ |
| Bull | White, Black spot | 20x25 | £12-£18 | $20-$30 | ☐ |
| Bull | White, Black spot/Yellow X | 20x25 | £12-£18 | $20-$30 | ☐ |
| Bull | White, Green hair, Green daisy/<br>Red Green L | 20x25 | £12-£18 | $20-$30 | ☐ |
| Bull | White, Green hair, Green heart/Blue<br>arrow, Orange heart/Green arrow | 20x25 | £12-£18 | $20-$30 | ☐ |
| Bull | White, Green hair, Orange/<br>Black daisy | 20x25 | £12-£18 | $20-$30 | ☐ |
| Bull | White, Green hair, red/Blue notes,<br>Orange heart/Blue arrow | 20x25 | £12-£18 | $20-$30 | ☐ |
| Bull | White, Green hair, red/Blue notes,<br>Red/Green L plates, | 20x25 | £12-£18 | $20-$30 | ☐ |
| Bull | White, Yellow hair, Blue/Green notes,<br>Blue heart/Yellow arrow, | 20x25 | £12-£18 | $20-$30 | ☐ |
| Bull | White, Yellow hair, Red heart/Blue<br>arrow, Red L | 20x25 | £12-£18 | $20-$30 | ☐ |
| Bull | White, Yellow hair, Blue/Yellow flower,<br>Red musical notes, Green lines, | 20x25 | £12-£18 | $20-$30 | ☐ |

## Cow: Series B – 1956-1958

*See picture on page 14 with Cats Series A*

| Item | Description | Size (mm) | Market Value | | Acquired |
|------|-------------|-----------|--------------|---|----------|
| Cow | White, Green ears, Orange daisy/<br>Blue daisy | 22x20 | £12-£18 | $20-$30 | ☐ |
| Cow | White, Green ears, Orange/Green<br>notes, Orange heart & Blue arrow | 22x20 | £12-£18 | $20-$30 | ☐ |
| Cow | White, Pink ears, Red flower, Red<br>heart/Green arrow | 22x20 | £12-£18 | $20-$30 | ☐ |
| Cow | White, Yellow ears, Orange/Blue<br>notes, Orange heart/Green arrow | 22x20 | £12-£18 | $20-$30 | ☐ |
| Cow | White, Yellow ears Red heart/<br>arrow, Yellow daisy | 22x20 | £12-£18 | $20-$30 | ☐ |
| Cow | White, Yellow ears, Blue daisy,<br>Orange L | 22x20 | £12-£18 | $20-$30 | ☐ |
| Cow | White, Yellow ears, Blue daisy,<br>Red/Blue notes | 22x20 | £12-£18 | $20-$30 | ☐ |
| Cow | White, Yellow ears, Green daisy,<br>Red flower | 22x20 | £12-£18 | $20-$30 | ☐ |
| Cow | White, Yellow ears, Blue heart/<br>Green arrow, Blue daisy | 22x20 | £12-£18 | $20-$30 | ☐ |

## Dog: Series C – 1957-1958

*See picture on page 16 with Bulls Series B*

| Item | Description | Size (mm) | Market Value | | Acquired |
|------|-------------|-----------|--------------|---|----------|
| Dog | White, Blue collar | 28x15 | £15-£18 | $20-$30 | ☐ |
| Dog | White, Orange flowers, Blue collar | 28x15 | £15-£18 | $20-$30 | ☐ |
| Dog | White, Red/Green collar | 28x15 | £15-£18 | $20-$30 | ☐ |
| Dog | White, Orange/Red flowers, no collar | 28x15 | £15-£18 | $20-$30 | ☐ |
| Dog | White, Red/Green collar | 28x15 | £15-£18 | $20-$30 | ☐ |
| Dog | White, Pink ears, Orange/Pink collar | 28x15 | £15-£18 | $20-$30 | ☐ |
| Dog | White, Yellow ears, Orange/ Yellow collar | 28x15 | £15-£18 | $20-$30 | ☐ |

## Donkey: Series C – 1957-1958

*See picture on page 16 with Bulls Series B*

| Item | Description | Size (mm) | Market Value | | Acquired |
|------|-------------|-----------|--------------|---|----------|
| Donkey | White, Green ears, Pink/Blue garland | 35x20 | £15-£18 | $20-$30 | ☐ |
| Donkey | White, Green ears Red flower | 35x20 | £15-£18 | $20-$30 | ☐ |
| Donkey | White, Pink ears, Red flower | 35x20 | £15-£18 | $20-$30 | ☐ |
| Donkey | White, Pink ears, Red/Yellow flower | 35x20 | £15-£18 | $20-$30 | ☐ |
| Donkey | White, Pink ears, Red/Yellow garland | 35x20 | £15-£18 | $20-$30 | ☐ |
| Donkey | White, Yellow ears, Red flower | 35x20 | £15-£18 | $20-$30 | ☐ |
| Donkey | White, Yellow ears, Pink/Blue garland | 35x20 | £15-£18 | $20-$30 | ☐ |
| Donkey | White, red/Yellow garland, Yellow eyes, | 35x20 | £15-£18 | $20-$30 | ☐ |

## Fawn: Series C – 1957-1958

*See picture on page 16 with Bulls Series B*

| Item | Description | Size (mm) | Market Value | | Acquired |
|------|-------------|-----------|--------------|---|----------|
| Fawn | White, Green ears, Yellow flower | 28x20 | £15-£18 | $20-$30 | ☐ |
| Fawn | White, Green ears, Yellow heart, Red arrow | 28x20 | £15-£18 | $20-$30 | ☐ |
| Fawn | White, Pink ears, Blue flowers/ heart/notes | 28x20 | £15-£18 | $20-$30 | ☐ |
| Fawn | White, Pink ears, Yellow flower | 28x20 | £15-£18 | $20-$30 | ☐ |
| Fawn | White, Pink ears, Yellow eyes, Yellow flower | 28x20 | £15-£18 | $20-$30 | ☐ |
| Fawn | White, Yellow ears, Blue flowers/ heart/notes | 28x20 | £15-£18 | $20-$30 | ☐ |
| Fawn | White, Yellow ears, Yellow eyes, Red flower | 28x20 | £15-£18 | $20-$30 | ☐ |

## Pelican: Series C – 1957-1958

| Item | Description | Size (mm) | Market Value | | Acquired |
|------|-------------|-----------|--------------|---|----------|
| Pelican | White, Blue wings, feet, anchor | 30x15 | £12-£18 | $20-$30 | ☐ |
| Pelican | White, Green wings, Blue anchor | 30x15 | £12-£18 | $20-$30 | ☐ |
| Pelican | White, Pink wings, feet, Blue anchor | 30x15 | £12-£18 | $20-$30 | ☐ |
| Pelican | White, Yellow wings, feet, Blue anchor | 30x15 | £12-£18 | $20-$30 | ☐ |
| Pelican | White, Green wings, Black waistcoat, Red tie | 30x15 | £12-£18 | $20-$30 | ☐ |

| | | | | | |
|---|---|---|---|---|---|
| Pelican | White, Pink wings, Black waistcoat, Red tie | 30x15 | £12-£18 | $20-$30 | ☐ |
| Pelican | White, Yellow wings, Black waistcoat, Red tie | 30x15 | £12-£18 | $20-$30 | ☐ |
| Pelican | White, Yellow wings, Blue waistcoat, Red tie | 30x15 | £12-£18 | $20-$30 | ☐ |

## DRUM BOX SERIES
**1957-1959**

| Item | Description | Size (mm) | Market Value | | Acquired |
|---|---|---|---|---|---|
| Harpy | Basset dog, Blue dress, mauve/ White harp | 45x28 | £40-£60 | $60-$90 | ☐ |
| Dora | Donkey, White dress, Yellow base | 55x25 | £70-£100 | $105-$155 | ☐ |
| Jem | Bulldog, eye patch, Grey trousers | 40x25 | £40-£60 | $60-$90 | ☐ |
| Clara | Cow, White dress, Brown cello | 50x25 | £40-£60 | $60-$90 | ☐ |
| Trunky | Elephant, Black tie | 50x35 | £50-£80 | $75-$120 | ☐ |

## NOVELTY MODELS
**1955-1960**

300

| Item | Description | Size (mm) | Market Value | | Acquired |
|---|---|---|---|---|---|
| Jumbo Jim | Elephant, Blue hat, tears | 45x25 | £100-£200 | $150-$305 | ☐ |
| Bernie & Poo | White/Brown; White/Blue | 55x75 | £70-£100 | $105-$155 | ☐ |
| Kitten on the Keys | Cat & Piano, Grey cat | 30x35 | £140-£160 | $205-$245 | ☐ |
| Kitten on the Keys | Cat & Piano, White | 30x35 | £140-£160 | $205-$245 | ☐ |
| Dustbin Cat | Cat in dustbin, Grey bin | 45x25 | £100-£150 | $150-$230 | ☐ |
| Jonah in the Whale | Blue jacket, White whale | 40x40 | £800-£1200 | $1195-$495 | ☐ |

## HORSE SETS
**Set 1 – 1974-1981**

300

| Item | Description | Size (mm) | Market Value | | Acquired |
|---|---|---|---|---|---|
| Mare | Dark Brown, lighter face | 76x76 | £8-£12 | $10-$20 | ☐ |
| Foal, Lying | Dark Brown, lighter face | 32x55 | £8-£12 | $10-$20 | ☐ |
| Foal, Standing | Dark Brown, lighter face | 48x48 | £8-£12 | $10-$20 | ☐ |
| Set of three | | | £25-£30 | $35-$45 | ☐ |

**Set 2 – 1978-1981**

| Item | Description | Size (mm) | Market Value | | Acquired |
|---|---|---|---|---|---|
| Mare | Honey, light Brown mane | 65x70 | £25-£30 | $35-$45 | ☐ |
| Foal, lying | Honey, light Brown mane | 30x46 | £25-£30 | $35-$45 | ☐ |
| Foal, standing | Honey, light Brown mane | 38x38 | £25-£30 | $35-$45 | ☐ |
| Set of three | | | £80-£120 | $120-$185 | ☐ |

# HAPPY FAMILIES

### Tiger Family – 1961-1965
This set was not reissued

| Item | Description | Size (mm) | Market Value | | Acquired |
|---|---|---|---|---|---|
| Mother | Beige | 40x40 | £30-£40 | $45-$60 | ☐ |
| Baby, sleeping | Beige | 10x30 | £28-£35 | $40-$55 | ☐ |
| Baby, awake | Biege | 10x30 | £28-£35 | $40-$55 | ☐ |
| Set of three boxed | | | £90-£120 | $135-$185 | ☐ |

### Giraffe Family: First issue – 1961-1965

| Item | Description | Size (mm) | Market Value | | Acquired |
|---|---|---|---|---|---|
| Mother | Beige, Blue eyes, light Grey horns | 60x45 | £12-£18 | $20-$30 | ☐ |
| Baby, sleeping | Beige, Blue eyes, light Grey horns | 15x30 | £8-£12 | $10-$20 | ☐ |
| Baby, awake | Beige, Blue eyes, light Grey horns | 40x38 | £8-£12 | $10-$20 | ☐ |
| Set of three boxed | | | £30-£40 | $45-$60 | ☐ |

### Giraffe Family: Second issue – 1978-1987

| Mother | Beige, Turquoise eyes, dark Grey horns | 60x45 | £12-£18 | $20-$30 | ☐ |
|---|---|---|---|---|---|
| Baby, sleeping | Beige, Turquoise eyes, dark Grey horns | 15x30 | £8-£12 | $10-$20 | ☐ |
| Baby, awake | Beige, Turquoise eyes, dark Grey horns | 40x28 | £8-£12 | $10-$20 | ☐ |
| Set of three boxed | | | £30-£40 | $45-$60 | ☐ |

## Hippo Family: First issue – 1961-1965

*28*

| Item | Description | Size (mm) | Market Value | | Acquired |
|------|-------------|-----------|--------------|---|----------|
| Mother | Blue eyes | 35x50 | £8-£12 | $10-$20 | ☐ |
| Baby asleep | Eyes shut | 20x25 | £5-£8 | $8-$10 | ☐ |
| Baby awake | Blue eyes | 28x25 | £5-£8 | $8-$10 | ☐ |
| Set of three boxed | | | £20-£25 | $30-$40 | ☐ |

## Hippo Family: Second issue – 1978-1987

| Item | Description | Size (mm) | Market Value | | Acquired |
|------|-------------|-----------|--------------|---|----------|
| Mother | Smoky Blue, tear | 35x50 | £5-£8 | $8-$10 | ☐ |
| Mother | Reddish Pink, White face | 28x65 | £5-£8 | $8-$10 | ☐ |
| Baby, asleep | Smoky Blue, tear | 20x25 | £5-£8 | $8-$10 | ☐ |
| Baby, awake | Smoky Blue, tear | 28x25 | £5-£8 | $8-$10 | ☐ |
| Baby, awake | Reddish Pink, White face | 28x65 | £5-£8 | $8-$10 | ☐ |
| Set of three boxed | | | £25-£30 | $35-$45 | ☐ |

## Mouse Family: First issue – 1962-1965

| Item | Description | Size (mm) | Market Value | | Acquired |
|------|-------------|-----------|--------------|---|----------|
| Mother | White, Pink ears, Yellow tails | 50x28 | £20-£25 | $30-$40 | ☐ |
| Baby, eyes closed | White, Pink ears, Yellow tails | 28x28 | £20-£30 | $30-$45 | ☐ |
| Baby, eyes open | White, Blue eyes, Yellow tails | 25x30 | £20-£30 | $30-$45 | ☐ |
| Set of three boxed | | | £60-£100 | $90-$155 | ☐ |
| Mother | White, Pink ears, Pink tails | 50x28 | £15-£20 | $20-$30 | ☐ |
| Baby, eyes closed | White, Pink ears, Pink tails | 28x28 | £10-£15 | $15-$25 | ☐ |
| Baby, eyes open | White, Blue eyes, Pink tails | 25x30 | £10-£15 | $15-$25 | ☐ |

## Rabbit Family: First issue – 1963-1965

| Item | Description | Size (mm) | Market Value | | Acquired |
|---|---|---|---|---|---|
| Mother | Turquoise | 55x30 | £20-£25 | $30-$40 | ☐ |
| Baby, Sitting | Turquoise | 34x28 | £20-£25 | $30-$40 | ☐ |
| Baby, Standing | Turquoise | 30x35 | £20-£30 | $30-$45 | ☐ |
| Set of three boxed | | | £60-£80 | $90-$120 | ☐ |

## Rabbit Family: Second issue – 1978-1984

| Item | Description | Size (mm) | Market Value | | Acquired |
|---|---|---|---|---|---|
| Mother | White, Blue patches | 55x30 | £8-£12 | $10-$20 | ☐ |
| Baby, sitting | White, Blue patches | 34x28 | £8-£12 | $10-$20 | ☐ |
| Baby, standing | White, Blue patches | 30x35 | £8-£12 | $10-$20 | ☐ |
| Set of three boxed | | | £25-£30 | $35-$45 | ☐ |

## Elephant Family – 1984-1987

36

| Item | Description | Size (mm) | Market Value | | Acquired |
|---|---|---|---|---|---|
| Mother | Blue, Pink ears | 35x70 | £8-£12 | $10-$20 | ☐ |
| Mother | Grey, Pink ears | 35x70 | £8-£12 | $10-$20 | ☐ |
| Baby, trunk up | Blue, Pink ears | 45x22 | £8-£12 | $10-$20 | ☐ |
| Baby, trunk up | Grey, Pink ears | 45x22 | £8-£12 | $10-$20 | ☐ |
| Baby, trunk down | Blue, Pink ears | 25x55 | £8-£12 | $10-$20 | ☐ |
| Baby, trunk down | Grey, Pink ears | 25x55 | £8-£12 | $10-$20 | ☐ |
| Set of three boxed | | | £25-£35 | $35-$55 | ☐ |

## Owl Family – 1984-1987

36

| Item | Description | Size (mm) | Market Value | | Acquired |
|---|---|---|---|---|---|
| Mother Owl | Cream | 40x40 | £10-£15 | $15-$25 | ☐ |
| Baby Owl, wings closed | Cream | 25x20 | £8-£12 | $10-$20 | ☐ |
| Baby Owl, wings open | Cream | 25x32 | £8-£12 | $10-$20 | ☐ |
| Set of three boxed | | | £30-£50 | $45-$75 | ☐ |

### Pig Family – 1984-1987

| Item | Description | Size (mm) | Market Value | | Acquired |
|---|---|---|---|---|---|
| Mother | Pink | 28x65 | £10-£15 | $15-$25 | ☐ |
| Mother | Reddish Pink, White face | 28x65 | £10-£15 | $15-$25 | ☐ |
| Baby Asleep | Pink, Blue eyes | 15x45 | £10-£15 | $15-$25 | ☐ |
| Baby Awake | Pink, Black eyes | 18x40 | £10-£15 | $15-$25 | ☐ |
| Baby Awake | Reddish Pink, White face | 18x40 | £10-£15 | $15-$25 | ☐ |
| Set of three boxed | | | £50-£80 | $75-$120 | ☐ |

### Frog Family – 1984-1987

44

| Item | Description | Size (mm) | Market Value | | Acquired |
|---|---|---|---|---|---|
| Mother | Brown, Red/Brown marks | 25x45 | £8-£12 | $10-$20 | ☐ |
| Baby smiling | Brown, Red/Brown marks | 20x30 | £5-£10 | $8-$15 | ☐ |
| Baby singing | Brown, Red/Brown marks | 25x25 | £8-£12 | $10-$20 | ☐ |
| Set of three boxed | | | £20-£30 | $30-$45 | ☐ |

### Mouse Family: Second issue – 1978-1987

| Mother | White, Grey markings | 50x28 | £8-£12 | $10-$20 | ☐ |
|---|---|---|---|---|---|
| Baby, eyes closed | White, Grey markings | 28x28 | £8-£12 | $10-$20 | ☐ |
| Baby, eyes open | White, Grey markings | 25x30 | £8-£12 | $10-$20 | ☐ |
| Set of three boxed | | | £20-£25 | $30-$40 | ☐ |

### Dog Family – 1987

39

| Item | Description | Size (mm) | Market Value | | Acquired |
|---|---|---|---|---|---|
| Mother | Brown, White face | 55x35 | £10-£15 | $15-$25 | ☐ |
| Puppy, standing | Brown, White face | 30x35 | £8-£12 | $10-$20 | ☐ |
| Puppy, lying | Brown, White face | 30x40 | £8-£12 | $10-$20 | ☐ |
| Set of three boxed | | | £25-£30 | $35-$45 | ☐ |

**Cat Family – 1987**

| Item | Description | Size (mm) | Market Value | | Acquired |
|---|---|---|---|---|---|
| Mother | Grey/White | 45x35 | £10-£15 | $15-$25 | ☐ |
| Kitten, Sitting | Grey/White | 30x20 | £8-£12 | $10-$20 | ☐ |
| Kitten, Lying | Grey/White | 30x35 | £8-£12 | $10-$20 | ☐ |
| Set of three boxed | | | £25-£30 | $35-$45 | ☐ |

# CHAMPIONSHIP DOGS – 1975-1981

| Item | Description | Size (mm) | Market Value | | Acquired |
|---|---|---|---|---|---|
| Afghan Hound | Beige/White | 85x90 | £40-£60 | $60-$90 | ☐ |
| Cocker Spaniel | Beige/Off White | 80x90 | £50-£80 | $75-$120 | ☐ |
| Collie | Honey | 85x85 | £50-£80 | $75-$120 | ☐ |
| English Setter | Beige | 80x90 | £50-£80 | $75-$120 | ☐ |
| Old English Sheepdog | Grey/White | 85x90 | £50-£80 | $75-$120 | ☐ |

# NURSERY FAVOURITES – 1972-1981

**Set 1: Dark Green boxes 1972**

| Item | Description | Size (mm) | Market Value | | Acquired |
|---|---|---|---|---|---|
| Jack | Green Trousers | 75x30 | £20-£25 | $30-$40 | ☐ |
| Jill | Green bonnet | 75x40 | £20-£25 | $30-$40 | ☐ |
| Little Miss Muffet | Yellow Hair | 60x50 | £20-£25 | $30-$40 | ☐ |
| Little Jack Horner | Green Jacket | 70x40 | £20-£25 | $30-$40 | ☐ |
| Humpty Dumpty | Honey Brown | 65x43 | £20-£25 | $30-$40 | ☐ |

**Set 2: Blue boxes 1973**

| Item | Description | Size (mm) | Market Value | | Acquired |
|---|---|---|---|---|---|
| Wee Willie Winkie | Yellow hair | 75x35 | £18-£25 | $30-$40 | ☐ |
| Mary Had a Little Lamb | Blue bonnet | 75x40 | £18-£25 | $30-$40 | ☐ |
| Polly Put the Kettle On | Pink cap | 75x35 | £25-£30 | $35-$45 | ☐ |
| Old King Cole | Yellow/Grey hat | 65x50 | £20-£25 | $30-$40 | ☐ |
| Tom Tom the Piper's Son | Grey hat | 65x55 | £20-£25 | $30-$40 | ☐ |

**Set 3: Yellow boxes 1974**

| Item | Description | Size (mm) | Market Value | Acquired | |
|---|---|---|---|---|---|
| Little Tommy Tucker | Yellow hair | 75x30 | £20-£25 | $30-$40 | ☐ |
| Mary Mary Quite Contrary | Yellow hair | 75x45 | £30-£35 | $45-$55 | ☐ |
| The Cat and the Fiddle | Brown/Grey | 70x50 | £25-£30 | $35-$45 | ☐ |
| The Queen of Hearts | Pink crown | 75x48 | £35-£40 | $50-$60 | ☐ |
| Little Boy Blue | Blue cap | 75x30 | £20-£25 | $30-$40 | ☐ |

**Set 4: Purple boxes 1976**

| Item | Description | Size (mm) | Market Value | Acquired | |
|---|---|---|---|---|---|
| Goosey Goosey Gander | Beige | 66x55 | £80-£120 | $120-$185 | ☐ |
| The Three Bears | Grey, Green base | 70x60 | £40-£45 | $60-$70 | ☐ |
| Little Bo Peep | Beige bonnet | 70x40 | £40-£45 | $60-$70 | ☐ |
| Old Woman Who Lived in a Shoe | Blue bonnet | 60x55 | £65-£85 | $95-$130 | ☐ |
| Puss in Boots | Beige, Blue boots | 70x30 | £25-£35 | $35-$55 | ☐ |

# WHIMSIE-LAND SERIES – 1984-1988

**Set 1: Pets – 1984**

| Item | Description | Size (mm) | Market Value | Acquired | |
|---|---|---|---|---|---|
| Pony | Grey mane | 37x47 | £8-£12 | $10-$20 | ☐ |
| Retriever | Beige | 32x60 | £8-£12 | $10-$20 | ☐ |
| Puppy | Beige | 35x36 | £8-£12 | $10-$20 | ☐ |
| Kitten | Grey, Blue wool | 20x42 | £10-£15 | $15-$25 | ☐ |
| Kitten | Grey, Pink wool | 20x42 | £8-£12 | $10-$20 | ☐ |
| Rabbit | Gold | 50x25 | £8-£12 | $10-$20 | ☐ |

**Set 2: Wildlife – 1984**

| Item | Description | Size (mm) | Market Value | Acquired | |
|---|---|---|---|---|---|
| Panda | Grey/White | 37x20 | £10-£15 | $15-$25 | ☐ |
| Lion | Brown | 30x50 | £10-£15 | $15-$25 | ☐ |
| Tiger | Brown/Orange | 22x50 | £10-£15 | $15-$25 | ☐ |
| Giraffe | Brown | 50x35 | £10-£15 | $15-$25 | ☐ |
| Elephant | Grey | 35x40 | £10-£15 | $15-$25 | ☐ |

**Set 3: Farmyard – 1985**

| Item | Description | Size (mm) | Market Value | Acquired | |
|---|---|---|---|---|---|
| Cockerel | Grey | 50x35 | £10-£20 | $15-$30 | ☐ |
| Duck | Grey | 45x35 | £10-£20 | $15-$30 | ☐ |
| Cow | Black & White | 30x45 | £15-£20 | $20-$30 | ☐ |
| Pig | Pink | 30x35 | £10-£20 | $15-$30 | ☐ |
| Goat | Pink | 35x35 | £10-£20 | $15-$30 | ☐ |

## Set 4: Hedgerow – 1986

| Item | Description | Size (mm) | Market Value | | Acquired |
|---|---|---|---|---|---|
| Hedgehog | Grey/Brown | 25x35 | £10-£20 | $15-$30 | ☐ |
| Badger | Grey | 25x35 | £10-£20 | $15-$30 | ☐ |
| Owl | White | 35x25 | £10-£20 | $15-$30 | ☐ |
| Squirrel | Grey | 35x25 | £10-£20 | $15-$30 | ☐ |
| Fox | Brown | 35x35 | £20-£25 | $30-$40 | ☐ |

## Set 5: British Wildlife – 1987

| Item | Description | Size (mm) | Market Value | | Acquired |
|---|---|---|---|---|---|
| Pheasant | Honey | 35x50 | £25-£30 | $35-$45 | ☐ |
| Field Mouse | Brown | 35x30 | £25-£30 | $35-$45 | ☐ |
| Partridge | White | 35x35 | £20-£25 | $30-$40 | ☐ |
| Otter | Brown | 40x40 | £20-£25 | $30-$40 | ☐ |
| Golden Eagle | Brown | 35x40 | £25-£30 | $35-$45 | ☐ |

# WHOPPAS

## Set 1: Red Box – 1976-1981

| Item | Description | Size (mm) | Market Value | | Acquired |
|---|---|---|---|---|---|
| Polar Bear | White | 35x55 | £10-£15 | $15-$25 | ☐ |
| Polar Bear | Beige | 35x55 | £10-£15 | $15-$25 | ☐ |
| Hippo | Grey | 35x50 | £10-£15 | $15-$25 | ☐ |
| Brown Bear | Brown | 35x45 | £10-£15 | $15-$25 | ☐ |
| Tiger | Yellow striped | 30x60 | £10-£15 | $15-$25 | ☐ |
| Elephant | Grey | 55x50 | £10-£15 | $15-$25 | ☐ |

## Set 2: Green box – 1977-1981

| Bobcat | Light Brown | 55x60 | £12-£18 | $20-$30 | ☐ |
|---|---|---|---|---|---|
| Chipmunk | Brown | 55x40 | £12-£18 | $20-$30 | ☐ |
| Racoon | Brown | 40x50 | £12-£18 | $20-$30 | ☐ |
| Bison | Brown | 40x50 | £12-£18 | $20-$30 | ☐ |
| Wolf | Grey | 60x45 | £12-£18 | $20-$30 | ☐ |

## Set 3: Brown Box – 1978-1981

| Item | Description | Size (mm) | Market Value | | Acquired |
|---|---|---|---|---|---|
| Otter | Brown | 30x55 | £20-£25 | $30-$40 | ☐ |
| Stoat | Brown | 35x55 | £20-£25 | $30-$40 | ☐ |
| Fox | Red/Brown | 30x60 | £20-£25 | $30-$40 | ☐ |
| Hedgehog | Brown | 30x50 | £20-£25 | $30-$40 | ☐ |
| Badger | Brown | 35x45 | £20-£25 | $30-$40 | ☐ |

# HAT BOX BOXES

# HAT BOX
## First Issue – 1956-1965
### Set One: Film: Lady & The Tramp

| Item | Description | Size (mm) | Market Value | | Acquired |
|------|-------------|-----------|--------------|---|----------|
| Tramp, standing | Grey/White | 50x50 | £30-£50 | $45-$75 | ☐ |
| Lady | Beige, Blue collar | 40x35 | £18-£25 | $30-$40 | ☐ |
| Peg | Yellow fringe | 40x35 | £18-£25 | $30-$40 | ☐ |
| Trusty | Brown nose | 55x35 | £25-£30 | $35-$45 | ☐ |
| Trusty | Black nose | 55x35 | £25-£30 | $35-$45 | ☐ |
| Jock | No coat | 40x25 | £25-£30 | $35-$45 | ☐ |
| Jock | Blue Tartan coat | 40x25 | £25-£30 | $35-$45 | ☐ |
| Jock | Green Tartan coat | 40x25 | £18-£25 | $30-$40 | ☐ |
| Scamp | Grey | 40x35 | £18-£25 | $30-$40 | ☐ |

### Set Two – Films: Bambi, Lady and the Tramp, Dumbo, Fantasia

| Item | Description | Size (mm) | Market Value | | Acquired |
|------|-------------|-----------|--------------|---|----------|
| Bambi | Beige | 40x35 | £12-£18 | $20-$30 | ☐ |
| Flower | Skunk, Black/White | 40x25 | £30-£50 | $45-$75 | ☐ |
| Dachie | Dog, Brown | 60x30 | £25-£40 | $35-$60 | ☐ |
| Toughy | Dog, Brown/White | 55x30 | £120-£180 | $180-$275 | ☐ |
| Baby Pegasus | Blue/Grey | 40x30 | £40-£60 | $60-$90 | ☐ |
| Am | Cat, eyes closed | 60x25 | £30-£40 | $45-$60 | ☐ |
| Si | Cat, eyes open | 60x30 | £30-£40 | $45-$60 | ☐ |
| Dumbo | Elephant, Grey/White | 40x38 | £35-£45 | $50-$70 | ☐ |
| Thumper | Rabbit Blue/Grey | 60x35 | £25-£35 | $35-$55 | ☐ |
| Thumper | Rabbit Blue/Grey – White cheeks | 60x35 | £25-£35 | $35-$55 | ☐ |

### Set Three – Films: 101 Dalmatians, The Sword in the Stone

| Item | Description | Size (mm) | Market Value | Acquired | |
|------|-------------|-----------|--------------|----------|---|
| The Colonel | Dog with Black streak to eye | 50x34 | £50-£80 | $75-$120 | ☐ |
| Girl Squirrel | Beige | 50x30 | £80-£120 | $120-$185 | ☐ |
| Sergeant Tibbs | Cat, beige | 55x30 | £50-£80 | $75-$120 | ☐ |
| Merlin as a Hare | Blue | 55x35 | £120-£180 | $180-$275 | ☐ |
| Archimedes | Owl, Brown | 50x35 | £80-£120 | $120-$185 | ☐ |
| Lucky | Dog, White Black spots | 30x35 | £60-£100 | $90-$155 | ☐ |
| Madam Mim | Hen, Brown | 30x28 | £120-£180 | $180-$275 | ☐ |
| Rolly | Dog, White, Black spots, Red collar | 40x30 | £60-£100 | $90-$155 | ☐ |
| Merlin as Turtle | Brown/Grey | 30x45 | £200-£300 | $295-$460 | ☐ |
| Merlin as Caterpillar | White/Pink/Mauve | 20x45 | £150-£200 | $220-$305 | ☐ |

**Second Issue – 1981-1985 – Films: Lady and the Tramp, Bambi, Fox and Hound**

| Item | Description | Size (mm) | Market Value | | Acquired |
|------|-------------|-----------|--------------|--|----------|
| Big Mama | Owl, Beige | 45x45 | £40-£50 | $60-$90 | ☐ |
| Tramp, sitting | Dog, Grey | 47x30 | £25-£30 | $35-$45 | ☐ |
| Copper | Dog, Beige, White chest/paws | 45x50 | £20-£25 | $30-$40 | ☐ |
| Dachie | Dog, light Brown | 60x30 | £15-£20 | $20-$30 | ☐ |
| Tod | Fox, Red/Brown | 45x50 | £40-£60 | $60-$90 | ☐ |
| Chief | Dog, Grey White chest | 50x20 | £20-£25 | $30-$40 | ☐ |
| Peg | Dog, Beige | 40x35 | £20-£25 | $30-$40 | ☐ |
| Scamp | Dog, Grey | 40x35 | £20-£25 | $30-$40 | ☐ |
| Lady | Dog, light Blue collar | 40x35 | £20-£25 | $30-$40 | ☐ |
| Bambi | Beige | 40x35 | £20-£25 | $30-$40 | ☐ |
| Jock | Dog, Green tartan coat | 40x25 | £20-£25 | $30-$40 | ☐ |
| Thumper | Rabbit, Grey | 60x35 | £20-£25 | $30-$40 | ☐ |

## HANNA-BARBERA CARTOON CHARACTERS

**Yogi Bear and Friends – 1962-1963**

| Item | Description | Size (mm) | Market Value | | Acquired |
|------|-------------|-----------|--------------|--|----------|
| Mr Jinks | Cat, Pink, Blue bowtie | 63x30 | £80-£120 | $120-$185 | ☐ |
| Mr Jinks | Cat, Yellow, Blue tie | 63x30 | £80-£120 | $120-$185 | ☐ |
| Huckleberry Hound | Dog, Blue, Yellow bowtie | 60x28 | £80-£120 | $120-$185 | ☐ |
| Yogi Bear | Bear, Red tie | 62x30 | £80-£120 | $120-$185 | ☐ |

*220*

## MGM CARTOON CHARACTERS

**Tom and Jerry – 1973-1979**

| Item | Description | Size (mm) | Market Value | | Acquired |
|------|-------------|-----------|--------------|--|----------|
| Tom | Cat, Blue | 90x55 | £40-£60 | $60-$90 | ☐ |
| Jerry | Mouse, Beige | 50x30 | £40-£60 | $60-$90 | ☐ |

*120*

# BENGO AND HIS PUPPY FRIENDS

**TV Pets – 1959-1965**

| Item | Description | Size (mm) | Market Value | | Acquired |
|------|-------------|-----------|--------------|------|----------|
| Whisky | Corgi, beige | 55x65 | £100-£150 | $150-$230 | ☐ |
| Chee-Chee | Pekinese beige | 60x35 | £35-£45 | $50-$70 | ☐ |
| Droopy Junior | Basset hound, Brown | 55x40 | £50-£80 | $75-$120 | ☐ |
| Fifi | Poodle, Grey/Blue | 55x35 | £25-£30 | $35-$45 | ☐ |
| Pepi | Chihuahua, tan patches | 55x35 | £40-£60 | $60-$90 | ☐ |
| Bruno Junior | St Bernard, Brown | 55x35 | £40-£60 | $60-$90 | ☐ |
| Mitzi | Kitten, Grey/Blue | 50x50 | £40-£60 | $60-$90 | ☐ |
| Percy | Afghan, beige | 65x30 | £60-£80 | $90-$120 | ☐ |
| Simon | Dalmatian, spotty | 60x40 | £30-£40 | $45-$60 | ☐ |
| Bengo | Boxer, light Brown | 55x50 | £40-£60 | $60-$90 | ☐ |

# TABBY CAT

| Item | Description | Size (mm) | Market Value | | Acquired |
|------|-------------|-----------|--------------|------|----------|
| Tabby | Brown stripes | 50x75 | £15-£20 | $20-$30 | ☐ |

# SHARPS CHOCOLATE

3⁰

## Smiling Rabbit
**Honey Brown Smiling Rabbit – 1970**

| Item | Description | Market Value | | Acquired |
|------|-------------|--------------|------|----------|
| Rabbit | Large Brown eyes | £25-£30 | $35-$45 | ☐ |
| Rabbit | Small Brown eyes | £25-£30 | $35-$45 | ☐ |

## Bo-Peep
**Honey Brown Bo-Peep – 1971**

| Bo-Peep | Brown | £25-£30 | $35-$45 | ☐ |
|---------|-------|---------|---------|---|
| Bo-Peep | Dark Blue hair, apron & flowers | £25-£30 | $35-$45 | ☐ |

3 0

## POS-NER ASSOCIATES
**Sherwood Forest – 1989-1995 – Ltd Edition of 5000**

| Item | Description | Size (mm) | Market Value | | Acquired |
|------|-------------|------|--------------|------|----------|
| Robin Hood | Green/Honey Brown | 70x30 | £20-£25 | $30-$40 | ☐ |
| Maid Marian | Grey-Blue/ Brown | 65x25 | £20-£25 | $30-$40 | ☐ |
| Friar Tuck | Red-Brown/ Honey | 45x30 | £20-£25 | $30-$40 | ☐ |

## ICI MAN
**(Imperial Chemical Industries) – Atromid-S Man**

| Item | Description | Market Value | | Acquired |
|------|-------------|--------------|------|----------|
| Small | Dark Blue all over- | £50-£80 | $75-$120 | ☐ |
| Small | Honey Brown all over- | £50-£80 | $75-$120 | ☐ |
| Large | Black all over | Very Rare | | ☐ |
| Large | Brown shirt, Red trousers | Very Rare | | ☐ |

## KING AQUARIUMS LTD
**1976-1980**

| Item | Description | (mm) | Market Value | | Acquired |
|------|-------------|------|--------------|------|----------|
| Seahorse | Blue/Beige | 70x30 | £120-£180 | $180-$275 | ☐ |
| Bridge | Beige | 45x80 | £70-£90 | $105-$140 | ☐ |
| Whelk/Water Snail | Honey Brown | 30x35 | £50-£80 | $75-$120 | ☐ |
| Mermaid | Beige | 60x58 | £35-£45 | $50-$70 | ☐ |
| Diver | Honey Brown | 70x28 | £20-£25 | $30-$40 | ☐ |
| Lighthouse | Beige | 75x45 | £35-£45 | $50-$70 | ☐ |
| Lighthouse | Honey Brown | 75x45 | £35-£45 | $50-$70 | ☐ |

## KP FOODS LTD
### KP Friars – 1983

| Item | Description | Size (mm) | Market Value | | Acquired |
|------|-------------|-----------|--------------|---|----------|
| Father Abbot | Beige | 45x18 | £12-£18 | $20-$30 | ☐ |
| Brother Peter | Beige | 40x18 | £12-£18 | $20-$30 | ☐ |
| Brother Peter | Honey | 40x18 | £12-£18 | $20-$30 | ☐ |
| Brother Benjamin | Beige | 40x18 | £12-£18 | $20-$30 | ☐ |
| Brother Crispin | Beige | 40x20 | £20-£25 | $30-$40 | ☐ |
| Brother Angelo | Beige | 48x20 | £20-£25 | $30-$40 | ☐ |
| Brother Francis | Beige | 42x20 | £20-£25 | $30-$40 | ☐ |
| Brother Francis | Honey | 42x20 | £20-£25 | $30-$40 | ☐ |

## PEX NYLONS
### Fairy and Candle Holder – Circa 1952

| Item | Description | Size (mm) | Market Value | | Acquired |
|------|-------------|-----------|--------------|---|----------|
| Fairy | Blue Wings | 55x35 | £250-£300 | $370-$460 | ☐ |
| Fairy | Pink Wings | 55x35 | £250-£300 | $370-$460 | ☐ |
| Fairy | Yellow Wings | 55x35 | £250-£300 | $370-$460 | ☐ |
| Fairy Holder | Pink/Green | 25x75 | £400-£600 | $590-$920 | ☐ |

## BALDING AND MANSELL
### Flintstones Christmas Cracker Premiums – 1965

| Item | Description | Size (mm) | Market Value | | Acquired |
|------|-------------|-----------|--------------|---|----------|
| Bluebird | Beige/Blue | 15x35 | £5-£8 | $8-$10 | ☐ |
| Crocodile | Brown/Green | 14x40 | £5-£8 | $8-$10 | ☐ |
| Hedgehog | Brown | 23x40 | £5-£8 | $8-$10 | ☐ |
| Terrapin | Beige | 10x40 | £5-£8 | $8-$10 | ☐ |
| Tiger | Yellow/Brown | 38x28 | £12-£18 | $20-$30 | ☐ |

| | | | | | |
|---|---|---|---|---|---|
| Dino | Beige | 35x35 | £12-£18 | $20-$30 | ☐ |
| Rhino | Beige | 20x40 | £12-£18 | $20-$30 | ☐ |
| Bronti | Brown | 20x35 | £12-£18 | $20-$30 | ☐ |

*For colourways of these see page ••.*

## KODIAK BEAR – CIRCA 1965

| Item | Description | Size (mm) | Market Value | | Acquired |
|---|---|---|---|---|---|
| Bear | Beige | 35x25 | £25-£30 | $35-$45 | ☐ |
| Bear | Brown | 40x25 | £25-£30 | $35-$45 | ☐ |
| Bear | Light Brown | 40x25 | £25-£30 | $35-$45 | ☐ |
| Bear | Red/Brown | 38x25 | £25-£30 | $35-$45 | ☐ |

## SPILLERS DOG FOODS LTD – 1991

| Item | Description | Size (mm) | Market Value | | Acquired |
|---|---|---|---|---|---|
| Retriever | Honey Brown | 26x53 | £18-£25 | $30-$40 | ☐ |

## ST BRUNO'S DOG KEYRING

| Item | Description | Market Value | | Acquired |
|---|---|---|---|---|
| Keyring | White/Brown | £20-£25 | $30-$40 | ☐ |

## FIREWORK PIG & ELEPHANT – CIRCA 1975

| Item | Description | Size (mm) | Market Value | | Acquired |
|---|---|---|---|---|---|
| Pig | White | 25x50 | £30-£40 | $45-$60 | ☐ |
| Elephant | Dark Grey | 27x35 | £30-£40 | $45-$60 | ☐ |

## SKIP THE DOG

| Description | Market Value | | Acquired |
|---|---|---|---|
| Came free with video | £8-£12 | $10-$20 | ☐ |

## WHITE SEAL ON ROCK

| Description | Market Value | | Acquired |
|---|---|---|---|
| Seal on Rock | £25-£30 | $35-$45 | ☐ |

## BRIGHTON CORPORATION
### Brighton Pavilion – 1988

| Item | Size (mm) | Market Valu | | Acquired |
|---|---|---|---|---|
| Oblong Pavilion | 50x53 | £10-£15 | $15-$25 | ☐ |
| Circular Pavilion | 75x53 | £10-£15 | $15-$25 | ☐ |

## LEVER REXONA
### Nursery Rhyme Models – 1970-1971

| Item | Market Value | | Acquired |
|---|---|---|---|
| Hickory Dickory Dock | £8-£12 | $10-$20 | ☐ |
| Gingerbread Man | £20-£25 | $30-$40 | ☐ |
| Humpty Dumpty | £8-£12 | $10-$20 | ☐ |
| Three Bears | £20-£25 | $30-$40 | ☐ |

| Item | Market Value | | Acquired |
|---|---|---|---|
| Old Woman Who Lived in a Shoe | £8-£12 | $10-$20 | ☐ |
| Doctor Foster | £8-£12 | $10-$20 | ☐ |
| Mary Mary Quite Contrary | £8-£12 | $10-$20 | ☐ |
| The House that Jack Built | £18-£25 | $30-$40 | ☐ |
| Red Riding Hood | £8-£12 | $10-$20 | ☐ |
| Jill | £8-£12 | $10-$20 | ☐ |

| Item | Market Value | | Acquired |
|---|---|---|---|
| Jack | £8-£12 | $10-$20 | ☐ |
| Mother Goose | £10-£15 | $15-$25 | ☐ |
| Goosey Goosey Gander | £8-£12 | $10-$20 | ☐ |
| Tom Tom the Pipers Son | £8-£12 | $10-$20 | ☐ |
| The Pied Piper | £8-£12 | $10-$20 | ☐ |
| Cat and the Fiddle | £10-£15 | $15-$25 | ☐ |

| Item | Market Value | | Acquired |
|---|---|---|---|
| Little Miss Muffet | £10-£15 | $15-$25 | ☐ |
| Little Jack Horner | £8-£12 | $10-$20 | ☐ |
| Puss in Boots | £8-£12 | $10-$20 | ☐ |
| Queen of Hearts | £8-£12 | $10-$20 | ☐ |
| Wee Willie Winkie | £10-£15 | $15-$25 | ☐ |
| Baa Baa Black Sheep | £20-£25 | $30-$40 | ☐ |
| Old King Cole | £8-£12 | $10-$20 | ☐ |

# TOM SMITH & CO LTD
## Circus – 1978-1979

| Item | | Size (mm) | Market Value | | Acquired |
|---|---|---|---|---|---|
| Elephant sitting | Blue | 35x30 | £5-£8 | $8-$10 | ☐ |
| Lion | Honey | 40x22 | £5-£8 | $8-$10 | ☐ |
| Sealion | Grey | 40x30 | £5-£8 | $8-$10 | ☐ |
| Pony | Beige | 45x22 | £5-£8 | $8-$10 | ☐ |
| Elephant standing | Blue | 30x25 | £5-£8 | $8-$10 | ☐ |
| Brown Bear | Brown | 35x30 | £5-£8 | $8-$10 | ☐ |

| Item | | Size (mm) | Market Value | | Acquired |
|---|---|---|---|---|---|
| Poodle | White | 30x35 | £5-£8 | $8-$10 | ☐ |
| Chimpanzee: | | | | | |
| Boy | Brown | 40x20 | £10-£15 | $15-$25 | ☐ |
| Boy | Beige | 40x20 | £5-£8 | $8-$10 | ☐ |
| Girl | Brown | 40x20 | £10-£15 | $15-$25 | ☐ |
| Girl | Beige | 40x20 | £5-£8 | $8-$10 | ☐ |

## Circus Models – 1993-1996

| Item | | Size (mm) | Market Value | | Acquired |
|---|---|---|---|---|---|
| Ringmaster | Light Grey | 44x20 | £5-£8 | $8-$10 | ☐ |
| Tiger | Honey Brown | 43x20 | £5-£8 | $8-$10 | ☐ |
| Tiger | Light Brown | 43x20 | £5-£8 | $8-$10 | ☐ |
| Clown Water Bucket | Light Green | 44x20 | £8-£12 | $10-$20 | ☐ |
| Clown Custard Pie | Pale Blue | 40x20 | £8-£12 | $10-$20 | ☐ |
| Strongman | Honey Brown | 40x20 | £8-£12 | $10-$20 | ☐ |
| Human Cannonball | Light Grey | 44x20 | £8-£12 | $10-$20 | ☐ |

# CLIFF RICHARD GUITAR BROOCH

| Item | Market Value | Acquired |
|---|---|---|
| Brooch | Rare | ☐ |

# WHITBREAD – HARRY THE FROG

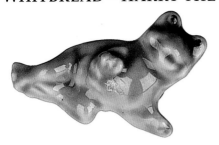

| Item | Market Value | | Acquired |
|------|-------------|--|----------|
| Frog | £30-£35 | $45-$55 | ☐ |

# THOMAS THE TANK ENGINE – 1986

| Item | Description | Size (mm) | Market Value | | Acquired |
|------|-------------|-----------|--------------|--|----------|
| Thomas the Tank Engine Miniature | | | | | |
| | Blue/Red | 28x40 | £80-£120 | $120-$185 | ☐ |
| Thomas the Tank Engine Money Box | | | | | |
| | Blue/Red | 110x165 | £150-£200 | $220-$305 | ☐ |
| Percy the Small Engine Money Box | | | | | |
| | Green/Red | 110x73 | £150-£200 | $220-$305 | ☐ |
| Percy the Small Engine Miniature | | | | | |
| | Green/Red | 28x38 | £80-£120 | $120-$185 | ☐ |

# SNOW WHITE & SEVEN DWARFS BROOCHES – 1938

| Item | Size (mm) | Market Value | Acquired |
|------|-----------|--------------|----------|
| Snow White | 40x10 | very rare | ☐ |
| Bashful | 35x10 | very rare | ☐ |
| Doc | 35x10 | very rare | ☐ |
| Grumpy | 38x10 | very rare | ☐ |
| Happy | 35x10 | very rare | ☐ |
| Sleepy | 35x10 | very rare | ☐ |
| Sneezy | 35x10 | very rare | ☐ |

# CLOSED EARED & OPENED EARED RABBIT
**Miniature Animals: 1967-1973**

| Description | Size (mm) | Market Value | | Acquired |
|-------------|-----------|--------------|--|----------|
| Gold Open eared Rabbit | 30x30 | £50-£100 | $75-$155 | ☐ |
| Beige Closed eared Rabbit | 30x30 | £10-£15 | $15-$25 | ☐ |

# THUNDER & LIGHTNING

| Item | Size(mm) | Market Value | | Acquired |
|------|----------|--------------|------|----------|
| Thunder | 25x33 | £10-£15 | $15-$25 | ☐ |
| Lightning | 25x33 | £10-£15 | $15-$25 | ☐ |

# BLACK POODLE

| Item | Description | Market Value | | Acquired |
|------|-------------|--------------|------|----------|
| Jenny | Black Poodle | £25-£30 | $35-$45 | ☐ |

# LEFTY & RIGHTY

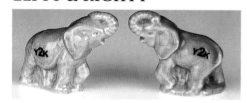

| Item | Market Value | | Acquired |
|------|--------------|------|----------|
| Lefty | £45-£50 | $65-$75 | ☐ |
| Righty | £15-£20 | $20-$30 | ☐ |

# TINIE TREASURES

| Item | Size (mm) | Market Value | | Acquired |
|------|-----------|--------------|------|----------|
| Lois Lane | 58 | £10-£15 | $15-$25 | ☐ |
| Supergirl | 58 | £10-£15 | $15-$25 | ☐ |
| Alfred | 58 | £10-£15 | $15-$25 | ☐ |
| Batman | 58 | £10-£15 | $15-$25 | ☐ |

# EURO DISNEY PROTOTYPES

| Item | Description | Size (mm) | Market Value | | Acquired |
|------|-------------|-----------|--------------|------|----------|
| Girl Squirrel | | 50x30 | £50-£80 | $75-$120 | ☐ |
| Big Mama | Owl | 45x45 | £50-£80 | $75-$120 | ☐ |
| The Colonel | Dog | 50x34 | £50-£80 | $75-$120 | ☐ |
| Flower | Skunk | 40x25 | £50-£80 | $75-$120 | ☐ |

# BEIGE/HONEY COLOURWAYS OF WHIMSIES

# BLUE COLOURWAYS OF WHIMSIES

# WHITE/OPAQUE COLOURWAYS OF WHIMSIES

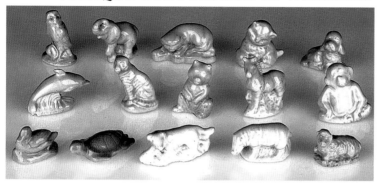

# GREEN COLOURWAYS OF WHIMSIES

# HEDGROW CRACKERS COLOURWAYS

| | Market Value | | Acquired |
|---|---|---|---|
| Each | £5-£8 | $8-$10 | ☐ |

# BALDING AND MANSELL
**Flintstones Christmas Cracker Premiums – 1965**
**Colourways**

# THE DINOSAUR COLLECTION – 1993
**Colourways**

# MIXED WHIMSIES
**Brown Colourways**

**Blue Colourways**

**Dark Blue Colourways**

**Orange/Brown Colourways**

**Beige/Honey Colourways**

Dark Brown Colourways

# THE DINOSAUR COLLECTION – 1993
Dark Blue and White Colourways

# AMERICAN ENDANGERED SPECIES COLOURWAYS

# SURVIVAL ANIMALS
## 1984-1985
### Armadillo Colourways

| Item | Description | Size (mm) | Market Value | | Acquired |
|------|-------------|-----------|--------------|---|----------|
| Pale Green | | 25x45 | £10-£20 | $15-$30 | ☐ |
| Gold | | 25x45 | £10-£20 | $15-$30 | ☐ |

# CIRCUS – 1978-1979
### Chimpanzee Boy Colourway

| Market Value | | Acquired |
|--------------|---|----------|
| £350-£400 | $520-$610 | ☐ |

# FAT CONTROLLER

| Market Value | | Acquired |
|--------------|---|----------|
| Prototype £350-£400 | $520-$610 | ☐ |

# MURRAY MINT COWBOY

| Item | Market Value | | Acquired |
|------|--------------|---|----------|
| Prototype | £400-£600 | $590-$920 | ☐ |

# BIRD LIFE SERIES – 1992-1993
### Barn Owl Colourway

| Market Value | | Acquired |
|--------------|---|----------|
| £350-£400 | $520-$610 | ☐ |

# CLARA COW

| Item | Market Value | | Acquired |
|------|--------------|---|----------|
| Prototype | £60-£100 | $90-$155 | ☐ |

# COLLIE DOG

| Item | Market Value | | Acquired |
|------|--------------|---|----------|
| Prototype | £200-£300 | $295-$460 | ☐ |

# DINOSAUR
**Original Colourway**

| Item | Market Value | Acquired | |
|---|---|---|---|
| Prototype | £75-£100 | $110-$155 | ☐ |

# CIBA GEIGY
**Toitoise – 1969 (Slow Fe)**

| Item | Description | Market Value | Acquired | |
|---|---|---|---|---|
| Slow Fe | Brown | £50-£80 | $75-$120 | ☐ |
| Slow K | Brown | £50-£80 | $75-$120 | ☐ |

# TOADSTOOL COTTAGE MONEY BOX

| Item | Market Value | Acquired | |
|---|---|---|---|
| Prototype | £250-£350 | $370-$535 | ☐ |

# POSY DUCK

| Market Value | Acquired | |
|---|---|---|
| £120-£150  $180-$230 | | ☐ |

# LARRY AND LESTER
**Leprechaun Twins: 1974-85**

| Item | Description | Market Value | Acquired | |
|---|---|---|---|---|
| Larry | Green hat | £40-£60 | $60-$90 | ☐ |
| Lester | Yellow hat | £40-£60 | $60-$90 | ☐ |

# CLIFF RICHARD PROTOTYPE PLAQUE

| Item | Market Value | Acquired | |
|---|---|---|---|
| Prototype | £100-£150 | $150-$230 | ☐ |

# ANGEL FISH PLAQUE

Rare

# BIRMINGHAM HARE PROTOTYPE
**Honey Colourway**

Rare

# SQUIRREL ASHTRAY

| Description | Market Value | Acquired | |
|---|---|---|---|
| Prototype | £60-£100 | $90-$155 | ☐ |

# NODDY SET DERIVATIVES
## Toadstool Cottage Money Box – Circa 1961

| Item | Description | Market Value | | Acquired |
|------|-------------|--------------|---|----------|
| Big Ears | Brown Roof with White spots | £200-£300 | $295-$460 | ☐ |
| Big Ears | Brown Roof with White spots/ Brown door | £200-£300 | $295-$460 | ☐ |
| Noddy | Brown Roof with White spots | £250-£300 | $370-$460 | ☐ |

# TV PETS

| Item | | Market Value | | Acquired |
|------|---|--------------|---|----------|
| Hollow Version | each | £65-£80 | $95-$120 | ☐ |

# KP FRIARS

| Item | Description | | Market Value | | Acquired |
|------|-------------|---|--------------|---|----------|
| Prototypes | Hollow Base | each | £20-£30 | $30-$45 | ☐ |

# BEAR AMBITIONS

| Item | Description | | Market Value | | Acquired |
|------|-------------|------|--------------|-----------|----------|
| Prototypes | Hollow Bases | each | £10-£15 | $15-$25 | ☐ |

# RACOON 1950s

| Item | Description | Size (mm) | Market Value | | Acquired |
|------|-------------|-----------|--------------|-----------|----------|
| Prototype | Hollow Base | | £75-£100 | $110-$155 | ☐ |

# THE NODDY SET: STYLE ONE – 1958-1961

| Item | Description | Size (mm) | Market Value | | Acquired |
|------|-------------|-----------|--------------|-----------|----------|
| Noddy | Red shirt, Blue hat | 70x35 | £180-£240 | $265-$365 | ☐ |
| Big Ears | Blue Jacket, Red hat | 70-35 | £120-£150 | $180-$230 | ☐ |
| Mr Plod | Blue uniform | 60x35 | £100-£150 | $150-$230 | ☐ |
| Miss Fluffy Cat | Brown Coat, Red bag | 60x35 | £80-£120 | $120-$185 | ☐ |

# LUCKY FAIRY FOLK:
**First version Brown faces – 1956-1960**

| Item | Description | Size (mm) | Market Value | | Acquired |
|------|-------------|-----------|--------------|--|----------|
| Leprechaun on Pig | Green hat | 45x35 | £35-£45 | $50-$70 | ☐ |
| Leprechaun on Pig | Orange hat | 45x35 | £35-£45 | $50-$70 | ☐ |
| Leprechaun on Pig | Red hat | 45x35 | £35-£45 | $50-$70 | ☐ |
| Leprechaun on Pig | Red hat White boots | 45x35 | £35-£45 | $50-$70 | ☐ |
| Pixie on Rabbit | Green hat | 40x32 | £55-£65 | $80-$100 | ☐ |
| Pixie on Rabbit | Red hat | 40x32 | £55-£65 | $80-$100 | ☐ |
| Pixie on Rabbit | Yellow hat | 40x32 | £55-£65 | $80-$100 | ☐ |
| Pixie on Acorn | Blue hat | 40x30 | £40-£45 | $60-$70 | ☐ |
| Pixie on Acorn | Green hat | 40x30 | £40-£45 | $60-$70 | ☐ |
| Pixie on Acorn | Orange hat | 40x30 | £40-£45 | $60-$70 | ☐ |
| Pixie on Acorn | Red hat | 40x30 | £40-£45 | $60-$70 | ☐ |
| Pixie on Acorn | Yellow hat | 40x30 | £40-£45 | $60-$70 | ☐ |
| Pixie on Acorn | White hat | 40x30 | £40-£45 | $60-$70 | ☐ |

# TAILOR AND COTTAGE ON IRISH BASE – 1970s

| Item | Description | Market Value | | Acquired |
|------|-------------|--------------|--|----------|
| Tailor | Blue Hat | £100-£150 | $150-$230 | ☐ |
| Tailor | Yellow Hat | £100-£150 | $150-$230 | ☐ |
| Tailor | Blue Hat & trousers | £100-£150 | $150-$230 | ☐ |

# IRISH RHINO DECANTER

| Item. | Market Value | | Acquired |
|---|---|---|---|
| Large | £325-£450 | $480-690 | ☐ |
| Medium | Rare | | ☐ |
| Small | £500-£700 | $740-1070 | ☐ |

# RHM FOODS OF ENGLAND
**Bisto Kids – 1977**

| Item | Description | Size (mm) | Market Value | | Acquired |
|---|---|---|---|---|---|
| Bisto Girl | Yellow hair | 115x48 | £60-£100 | $90-$155 | ☐ |
| Bisto Boy | Red hair | 110x58 | £60-£100 | $90-$155 | ☐ |
| Set of 2 | | | £120-£200 | $180-$305 | |

# PROTOTYPE PLAQUES

| Rare | ☐ |
|---|---|

# ALPHABET AND LONDON TRAINS

Colourways & Prototypes 1958-1961

# GOLDILOCKS AND THE THREE BEARS – 1953-1958

| Item | Description | Size (mm) | Market Value | | Acquired |
|------|-------------|-----------|--------------|-----|----------|
| Goldilocks | Blonde hair | 100x60 | £300-£400 | $445-$610 | ☐ |
| Poppa Bear | Light Brown | 95x30 | £300-£400 | $445-$610 | ☐ |
| Mama Bear | Light Brown | 100x65 | £300-£400 | $445-$610 | ☐ |
| Baby Bear | Brown | 50x30 | £300-£400 | $445-$610 | ☐ |

# MICKEY MOUSE – 1935

| Description | Market Value | | Acquired |
|-------------|--------------|-----|----------|
| Yellow hands and shoes | £1500-£2000 | $2220-$3060 | ☐ |
| Yellow hands, Green shorts and Orange shoes | £1500-£2000 | $2220-$3060 | ☐ |
| Yellow hands, Blue shorts and Orange shoes | £1500-£2000 | $2220-$3060 | ☐ |
| Yellow hands, Orange shorts and shoes | £1500-£2000 | $2220-$3060 | ☐ |

# THE BUTCHER, THE BAKER AND THE CANDLESTICK MAKER – 1953-1958

| Item | Description | Size (mm) | Market Value | | Acquired |
|---|---|---|---|---|---|
| Butcher | Blue/White apron, Grey trousers | 95x40 | £250-£350 | $370-$535 | ☐ |
| Baker | Blue/White shirt, Blue trousers | 95x30 | £250-£350 | $370-$535 | ☐ |
| Baker | White Shirt | 95x30 | £250-£350 | $370-$535 | ☐ |
| Candlestick Maker | Yellow candlestick | 110x25 | £300-£400 | $445-$610 | ☐ |
| Candlestick Maker | Beige candlestick, Black coat | 110x25 | £300-£400 | $445-$610 | ☐ |
| Candlestick Maker | Beige candlestick, Green coat | 110x25 | £300-£400 | $445-$610 | ☐ |

# COMIC RABBIT (LITTLE LAUGHING RABBIT) – 1948 –1952

| Description | Size (mm) | Market Value | | Acquired |
|---|---|---|---|---|
| Pale Grey, Black eyes | 63x38 | £60-£100 | $90-$155 | ☐ |
| Pale Grey, Red eyes | 63x38 | £60-£100 | $90-$155 | ☐ |
| White | 63x38 | £60-£100 | $90-$155 | ☐ |
| Dark Grey | 63x38 | £60-£100 | $90-$155 | ☐ |
| Beige | 63x38 | £60-£100 | $90-$155 | ☐ |
| Dark Grey, Black eyes | 63x38 | £60-£100 | $90-$155 | ☐ |
| Pale Grey, Red mouth | 63x38 | £60-£100 | $90-$155 | ☐ |
| Pale Grey, striped ears | 63x38 | £60-£100 | $90-$155 | ☐ |
| Pink | 70x40 | £60-£100 | $90-$155 | ☐ |
| White | 65x40 | £60-£100 | $90-$155 | ☐ |

# COMIC PENGUIN FAMILY – 1948-1955

| Item | Description | Size (mm) | Market Value | | Acquired |
|---|---|---|---|---|---|
| Mr Penquin | White/Grey Pale Blue cap | 90x40 | £100-£150 | $150-$230 | ☐ |
| Mr Penquin | White, Blue cap | 90x40 | £100-£150 | $150-$230 | ☐ |
| Mr Penquin | Black/White, Blue cap | 90x40 | £100-£150 | $150-$230 | ☐ |
| Mrs Penquin | White/Grey | 85x40 | £100-£150 | $150-$230 | ☐ |
| Benny | White/Grey, Blue tam | 55x25 | £100-£150 | $150-$230 | ☐ |
| Penny | White/Grey, Blue bonnet | 50x25 | £100-£150 | $150-$230 | ☐ |
| Mr Penquin Pepper Pot | Maroon cap | 90x40 | £100-£150 | $150-$230 | ☐ |
| Mr Penquin Pepper Pot | Blue cap | 65x40 | £100-£150 | $150-$230 | ☐ |
| Mr Penquin Pepper Pot | Pale Green | 75x40 | £150-£180 | $220-$275 | ☐ |
| Mrs Penquin Salt Pot | Maroon shawl | 85x40 | £100-£150 | $150-$230 | ☐ |
| Mrs Penquin Salt Pot | Pale Green | 65x40 | £150-£180 | $150-$275 | ☐ |

## COMIC RABBIT SALT AND PEPPER POTS – 1948

| Item | Size (mm) | Market Value | | Acquired |
|---|---|---|---|---|
| Mr Rabbit Salt Pot Yellow jacket | 90x40 | £70-£100 | $105-$155 | ☐ |
| Mrs Rabbit Pepper Pot Maroon hat | 90x40 | £70-£100 | $105-$155 | ☐ |
| Set of 2 with tray | | very rare | | ☐ |

## ABC CATS – 1930-1955

| Description | Market Value | | Acquired |
|---|---|---|---|
| Various colourways | £40-£60 | $60-$90 | ☐ |

## IRISH POLAR BEAR – 1970s

| Market Value | | Acquired |
|---|---|---|
| £500-£700 | $740-$1070 | ☐ |

## KISSING BUNNIES – 1948-1950s

| Description | Size (mm) | Market Value | | Acquired |
|---|---|---|---|---|
| White/Grey bunny, large eyes | 64x80 | £80-£120 | $120-$185 | ☐ |
| White/beige bunny, large eyes | 64x80 | £80-£120 | $120-$185 | ☐ |
| White/Brown bunny, small eyes | 64x80 | £80-£120 | $120-$185 | ☐ |
| White/Grey bunny, White tail | 64x80 | £80-£120 | $120-$185 | ☐ |
| White/Grey bunny, Grey tail | 64x80 | £80-£120 | $120-$185 | ☐ |

## INDIAN RUNNER DUCKS – 1932-1953

| Item | Description | Market Value | | Acquired |
|---|---|---|---|---|
| Mother Duck | Blue/Grey/White | £40-£60 | $60-$90 | ☐ |
| Duckling head up | White | £40-£60 | $60-$90 | ☐ |
| Duckling head down | White | £40-£60 | $60-$90 | ☐ |

# HIGH GLOSS MODELS

## Kid –1930-1950

| Item | Description | Market Value | | Acquired |
|------|-------------|--------------|--|----------|
| Kid | Beige | £60-£80 | $90-$120 | ☐ |
| Kid | Off White | £60-£80 | $90-$120 | ☐ |

## Squirrel – 1930-1955

| Item | Description | Market Value | | Acquired |
|------|-------------|--------------|--|----------|
| Squirrel sitting | Red/Brown | £50-£80 | $75-$120 | ☐ |
| Squirrel sitting | Light Brown | £50-£80 | $75-$120 | ☐ |
| Squirrel sitting | Light Grey | £50-£80 | $75-$120 | ☐ |
| Squirrel sitting | Light Grey/White | £50-£80 | $75-$120 | ☐ |
| Squirrel lying | Red/Brown | £60-£80 | $90-$120 | ☐ |
| Squirrel lying | Beige | £60-£80 | $90-$120 | ☐ |

## Rabbits – 1930-1955

| Item | Description | Market Value | | Acquired |
|------|-------------|--------------|--|----------|
| Bunny | White, light Brown markings | £30-£40 | $45-$60 | ☐ |
| Bunny | Brown | £30-£40 | $45-$60 | ☐ |
| Bunny | White, light Grey markings | £30-£40 | $45-$60 | ☐ |
| Double Bunnies | White/Grey markings | £30-£40 | $45-$60 | ☐ |
| Double Bunnies | Brown/White markings | £30-£40 | $45-$60 | ☐ |
| Double Bunnies | White/pale Grey markings | £30-£40 | $45-$60 | ☐ |
| Double Bunnies | White/Grey markings – medium | £40-£50 | $60-$75 | ☐ |
| Double Bunnies | White/Grey markings– large | £50-£80 | $75-$120 | ☐ |
| Double Bunnies | White/Grey markings, Pink ears – large | £50-£80 | $75-$120 | ☐ |
| Double Bunnies | White/Grey tail | £50-£80 | $75-$120 | ☐ |

## Elephant – 1930-1950

| Item | Description | Market Value | | Acquired |
|------|-------------|--------------|--|----------|
| Elephant | Pale Grey | £80-£120 | $120-$185 | ☐ |

## Foals – 1930-1953

| Item | Description | Market Value | | Acquired |
|------|-------------|--------------|---|----------|
| Head back | Beige-Large | £50-£80 | $75-$120 | ☐ |
| Head back | White- Med | £40-£60 | $60-$90 | ☐ |
| Head back | Beige-Small | £30-£50 | $45-$75 | ☐ |
| Head down | White | £45-£55 | $65-$85 | ☐ |
| Head down | Beige | £45-£55 | $65-$85 | ☐ |

## Foals – 1948-1953

| Item | Description | Market Value | | Acquired |
|------|-------------|--------------|---|----------|
| Foal rear leg forward | Light Brown | £60-£80 | $90-$120 | ☐ |
| Foal rear leg forward | White | £60-£80 | $90-$120 | ☐ |
| Foal rear leg | White, forward Blue mane | £60-£80 | $90-$120 | ☐ |
| Foal rear leg forward | Dark Brown | £60-£80 | $90-$120 | ☐ |
| Foal | White | £60-£80 | $90-$120 | ☐ |
| Foal | Dark Brown | £60-£80 | $90-$120 | ☐ |

## Panda – 1930s

| Item | Description | Market Value | | Acquired |
|------|-------------|--------------|---|----------|
| Panda | Large | £900-£1200 | $1330-$1835 | ☐ |
| Panda | Med | £700-£900 | $1035-$1375 | ☐ |
| Panda | Small | £400-£600 | $590-$920 | ☐ |

## Monkey – 1930

| Item | Description | Market Value | | Acquired |
|------|-------------|--------------|---|----------|
| Monkey | Light Brown | £200-£300 | $295-$460 | ☐ |

## Fawn – 1938

| Item | Description | Market Value | | Acquired |
|------|-------------|--------------|---|----------|
| Facing right | Beige/light markings | £50-£80 | $75-$120 | ☐ |
| Facing right | Beige/dark markings | £50-£80 | $75-$120 | ☐ |
| Facing right | White | £50-£80 | $75-$120 | ☐ |
| Facing left | Off White | £50-£80 | $75-$120 | ☐ |
| Facing left | Off White/Grey | £50-£80 | $75-$120 | ☐ |

## Spaniel – 1935-1939

| Item | Description | Market Value | | Acquired |
|---|---|---|---|---|
| Seated | White, Black markings | £180-£240 | $265-$365 | ☐ |
| Seated | White, Brown markings | £180-£240 | $265-$365 | ☐ |

## Pandas – 1939

| Item | Description | Market Value | | Acquired |
|---|---|---|---|---|
| Panda walking | Black & White | £200-£300 | $295-$460 | ☐ |
| Panda sitting | Black & White | £200-£300 | $295-$460 | ☐ |

## Panther – 1939

| Description | Market Value | | Acquired |
|---|---|---|---|
| Light Brown, Green tree trunk base | £700-£1000 | $1035-$1530 | ☐ |

## Ermine – 1939

| Description | Market Value | | Acquired |
|---|---|---|---|
| White, Blue/Grey base | £1700-£2400 | $2515-$3670 | ☐ |

## Puppies – 1948-1953

| Item | Description | Market Value | | Acquired |
|---|---|---|---|---|
| Puppy begging | White | £40-£60 | $60-$90 | ☐ |
| Puppy with slipper | White | £40-£60 | $60-$90 | ☐ |

## Hoopee Bird – 1930s

| Description | Market Value | | Acquired |
|---|---|---|---|
| Yellow/Blue, tree trunk base | £1500-£2000 | $2220-$3060 | ☐ |

## Budgerigars – 1939-1955

| Item | Description | Market Value | | Acquired |
|---|---|---|---|---|
| Style one | Pale Blue, Blue/Green base | £200-£300 | $295-$460 | ☐ |
| Style one | Yellow, Brown/Green base | £200-£300 | $295-$460 | ☐ |
| Style one | Yellow, Green wings | £200-£300 | $295-$460 | ☐ |
| Style two | Pale Green, flower to branch | £200-£300 | $295-$460 | ☐ |
| Style two | Pale Blue, flower to branch | £200-£300 | $295-$460 | ☐ |
| Budgerigars | Yellow/Blue/Green bird | £200-£300 | $295-$460 | ☐ |
| Budgerigars | Yellow bird,Green tail/Green bird | £200-£300 | $295-$460 | ☐ |

## Parrot – 1939

| Item | Description | Market Value | | Acquired |
|---|---|---|---|---|
| Parrot on Tree Stump | Blue head, fawn stump | £1200-£1800 | $1775-$2755 | ☐ |

## Heron – 1946-1953

| Description | Market Value | | Acquired |
|---|---|---|---|
| Dark Blue/Grey | £800-£1200 | $1185-$1835 | ☐ |

## Woodpecker – 1946-1953

| Description | Market Value | | Acquired |
|---|---|---|---|
| Off White, Maroon head | £250-£300 | $370-$460 | ☐ |

## Goldfinches – 1939-1955

| Item | Market Value | | Acquired |
|------|--------------|---|----------|
| Goldfinches | £200-£300 | $295-$460 | ☐ |

## Cockatoo – 1939-1955

| Item | Description | Market Value | | Acquired |
|------|-------------|--------------|---|----------|
| Cockatoo | White, Yellow crest | £500-£700 | $740-$1070 | ☐ |
| Cockatoo | White, Pink crest | £500-£700 | $740-$1070 | ☐ |
| Cockatoo | White, bright Pink crest | £500-£700 | $740-$1070 | ☐ |

## WILDFOWL WALL PLAQUES – 1960s

| Item | Market Value | | Acquired |
|---|---|---|---|
| Mallard | £175-£200 | $260-$305 | ☐ |
| Shoveller | £375-£500 | $555-$765 | ☐ |
| Pintail | £375-£500 | $555-$765 | ☐ |

# THE WORLD OF SURVIVAL SERIES
## 1976-1982
### Set One

| Item | Description | Size (mm) | Market Value | | Acquired |
|---|---|---|---|---|---|
| African Elephant | Grey, White tusks | 160x260 | £300-£400 | $445-$610 | ☐ |
| African Lion | Brown | 110x200 | £200-£400 | $295-$610 | ☐ |
| American Bison | Dark Brown | 120x190 | £200-£300 | $295-$460 | ☐ |
| Black Rhino | Light Grey | 110x240 | £300-£400 | $445-$610 | ☐ |
| Polar Bear | White | 110x210 | £250-£350 | $370-$535 | ☐ |
| Tiger | Orange | 95x190 | £200-£300 | $295-$460 | ☐ |

### Set Two

| Item | Description | Size (mm) | Market Value | | Acquired |
|---|---|---|---|---|---|
| African Cape Buffalo | Brown | 170x240 | £600-£700 | $890-$1070 | ☐ |
| American Brown Bear | Dark Brown | 105x145 | £200-£300 | $295-$460 | ☐ |
| American Cougar | Beige | 150x225 | £300-£400 | $445-$610 | ☐ |
| Harp Seal & Pup | Off White | 85x220 | £600-£700 | $890-$1070 | ☐ |
| Hippo | Brown | 105x220 | £300-£400 | $445-$610 | ☐ |
| Mountain Gorilla | Black | 150x150 | £300-£400 | $445-$610 | ☐ |

# PLUTO – 1937-1938

| Item | Description | Market Value | | Acquired |
|------|-------------|--------------|--|----------|
| Pluto | Orange/Brown | £400-£600 | $590-$920 | ☐ |
| Pluto | Grey | £400-£600 | $590-$920 | ☐ |

# STORY BOOK FIGURES
## Alice and the Dodo: 1935-1938

| Description | Market Value | | Acquired |
|-------------|--------------|--|----------|
| Orange/Yellow dress, light Brown bird | £500-£800 | $740-$1225 | ☐ |
| Green dress, dark Brown bird | £500-£800 | $740-$1225 | ☐ |
| Pink dress, dark Brown bird | £500-£800 | $740-$1225 | ☐ |
| Blue dress, dark Brown bird | £500-£800 | $740-$1225 | ☐ |

# SMURFS PROTOTYPES

| Item | Market Value | | Acquired |
|------|--------------|--|----------|
| Each | £300-£400 | $445-$610 | ☐ |

# 1950s FLEUR DE LYS POT AND COVER

| Item | Market Value | | Acquired |
|------|--------------|--|----------|
| Fleur De Lys Pot and Cover | £100-£200 | $150-$305 | ☐ |

# BLUE SCOTTIE DOG

| Item | Market Value | Acquired |
|------|--------------|----------|
| One off | Very Rare | ☐ |

# DUCKS – 1932-1953

Large, medium and small sizes, various colourways

| Description | Market Value | | Acquired |
|---|---|---|---|
| Duck head forward | £50-£80 | $75-$120 | ☐ |
| Duck head back | £50-£80 | $75-$120 | ☐ |
| Duck preening | £50-£80 | $75-$120 | ☐ |
| Duck pecking | £50-£80 | $75-$120 | ☐ |
| Duck open wings | £50-£80 | $75-$120 | ☐ |

# DISNEY BLOW UPS – 1961-1965

| Item | Description | Size (mm) | Market Value | | Acquired |
|---|---|---|---|---|---|
| Scamp | Grey | 110x115 | £130-£180 | $190-$275 | ☐ |
| Bambi | Beige | 110x120 | £130-£180 | $190-$275 | ☐ |
| Tramp | Grey | 160x105 | £200-£300 | $295-$460 | ☐ |
| Dachie | Beige | 125x105 | £500-£600 | $740-$890 | ☐ |
| Thumper | Blue | 130x80 | £250-£350 | $370-$535 | ☐ |
| Lady | Beige | 110x140 | £175-£250 | $260-$385 | ☐ |
| Si | Brown | 140x110 | £180-£240 | $265-$365 | ☐ |
| Am | Brown, teeth | 147x85 | £180-£240 | $265-$365 | ☐ |
| Trusty | Beige | 135x80 | £175-£250 | $260-$385 | ☐ |
| Jock | Grey | 100x115 | £500-£800 | $740-$1225 | ☐ |

# EURO DISNEY

**Snow White and Seven Dwarfs Prototype** (5 Dwarfs Pictured)

| Item | Market Value | | Acquired |
|---|---|---|---|
| Prototype | £800-£1200 | $1185-$1835 | ☐ |

# SONIA FACE MASK

| Market Value | | Acquired |
|---|---|---|
| £600-£1000 | $890-$1530 | ☐ |

# FROLIC FACE MASK

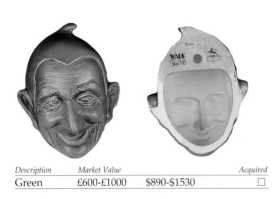

| Description | Market Value | | Acquired |
|---|---|---|---|
| Green | £600-£1000 | $890-$1530 | ☐ |

# CELLULOSE FIGURES
## Curtsey: 1927-1939

| Item | Market Value | | Acquired |
|---|---|---|---|
| Various Colourways | £80-£120 | $120-$185 | ☐ |

## Sunshine: 1927-1939

| Item | Market Value | | Acquired |
|---|---|---|---|
| Various colourways | £200-£300 | $295-$460 | ☐ |

## Sleepyhead: 1927-1939

| Item | Market Value | | Acquired |
|---|---|---|---|
| Two colourways | £700-£900 | $1035-$1375 | ☐ |

## Lady Seated on Chaise

| Item | Market Value | | Acquired |
|---|---|---|---|
| Seated figure | £600-£800 | $890-$1225 | ☐ |

*Large and small Alsatian, designed by Jessie Van Hallen, 10¼ins high and 4¾ ins high respectively.*

*A group of figures by* Jessie Van Hallen. *Front:* **Strawberry Girl**, **Tessa**, **Anton**, **Alice**. *Middle:* **Carnival**, **Elf 2**, **Humoresque**. *Top:* **Pompadour**, **Bride**, **Curtsey**. *To find any of these figures on their original lamp bases is very unusual and will certainly add to the value. One point worth noting is that only a maximum of 40 watts should be used in these figurative lamps, preferably less, so that the cellulose coating can be maintained.*

*A group of 'Scintillite' coated figures by Jessie Van Hallen, including;* **Daisette**, **Christina**, **Carmen**, **Helga**, **Argentina** *and* **Gloria** *in the centre. The tallest figure in this group is Christina at about 11ins high.*

*A group of figures by* Jessie Van Hallen. *Front:* **Zena**, *two small figures of* **Jose**, **Rhythm**. *Top:* **Cherry**, **Pavlova**, **Cherry**, *unknown. Again notice the colour variations of the duplicates. (See listings for details)*

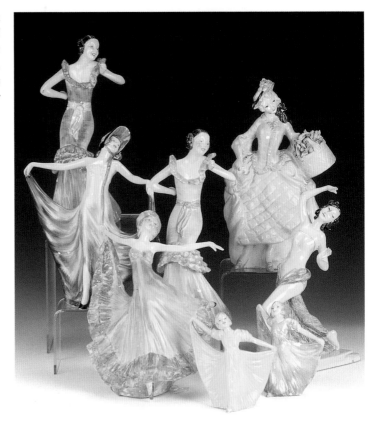

A group of figures by Jessie Van Hallen. Front: **Zena**, two **Sunshine** and two **Curtsey**. Top: unknown, **Grace**, **Mimi** and two figures of **Springtime**. One of the most obvious features of these figures is the relative freedom of colours that could be used. This is particularly noticeable on the duplicate figures. It is also worth noting that the figure of Springtime is very similar to a figure called Greta, the former having a larger rocky base compared to the smaller and smoother base of Greta. Some of these late 1920s Jessie Van Hallen figures were later made using underglaze colours and fired. The value of these is usually higher than their respective cellulose figure. (See listings for details)

A group of figures by Jessie Van Hallen. Front: **Barbara**, **Jeanette**, two figures of **Snow White**, **Jeanette**. Middle: two figures of **Romance**. Top: **Sadie** and **Lotus**.

*Snow White and The Seven Dwarfs* (Disney Characters copyright The Walt Disney Company) 1938. Designed by Jessie Van Hallen. Snow White 6¼ ins high and the dwarfs from 3½ ins to 4 ins high.

A collection of **animal figurines** dating from the 1930s and 1940s. These are very similar, sometimes identical to animals made by other potteries such as Shaw & Copestake, Sylvac Works and the Price Bros. of Burslem. In the late 1940s and 1950s Wadeheath used up surplus stock of the smaller animals by placing them on bases with miniature flower vases.

A collection of money boxes – **Peter the Polar Bear**, 1988, **Bambi**. The **Natwest Seated Panda**, 1989, and the **Thorntons Chocolate Wagon**.

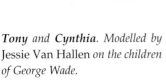

**Tony** and **Cynthia**. Modelled by Jessie Van Hallen *on the children of George Wade.*

A collection of **Walt Disney character children's teapots and cups**. The teapots are about 3½ inches high.

A collection of **moulded jugs** dating from the 1930s and 1940s. Including a **'Lambeth Walk'** pitcher (top right), circa 1939, many of which were produced as musical versions.

A collection of **Royal Commemorative wares** related to the coronation of Queen Elizabeth II, 2nd June, 1953.

*A moulded biscuit box and cover and a cheese dish and cover with bird finials. Late 1930s. **Pig family cruet set** and a **Rabbit family cruet set**, 1940's, both formerly individual figures.*

*A very rare sample of the **Snow White tableware set** produced in 1938 to coincide with the new animated Walt Disney movie.*

*A part **Snow White and the Seven Dwarfs children's tea set** dating from about 1938. Yet another product relating to the new Walt Disney picture, Wade Heath & Co. having been granted the sole production rights for using Walt Disney characters on their products in 1934.*

*Nursery Rhyme Figures*. From left to right – **Blyken**, **Wyken**, **Nod**. This shows both types of figure with the 1948-52 models with flowers on the base in the front and the 1952-58 version without the flowers.

*Nursery Rhyme Figures*. From left to right – **Poorman**, **Tinker**, **Tailor** and the two versions of **I've a Bear Behind**.

*A set of four* **Guinness promotional figurines**, *1968. These had a limited issue making the figures quite sought after.*

*500*

*Bottom left:* **The Whimsies British Character set**, *1959, of the* **Pearly King and Queen**, *a* **Fishmonger** *and a* **Lawyer**. *Three of the five comical novelty animal sets dating from 1955-60 with the Irish Wade* **'Pex' Fairy** *promotional figure made for Pex stockings between 1948-50. Later incorporated onto a candle holder.* **Kissing Rabbits**, *1930s. Beware of an identical pair, unmarked, not made by Wade.* **Standing Rabbits** *also from the 1930s. The last two being slip-cast under glazed figures. Middle: The Walt Disney characters from* **The Sword and the Stone**, *'Hat Box' Series made between 1956-65 with,* **Madam Mim (Hen)**, **Archimedes (Owl)**, **Merlin as Hare**, **The Girl Squirrel**, **Merlin as Caterpillar** *and* **Merlin as Turtle**. *Top: The* **Aquarium Set** *dating from 1975-80 with the only piece missing being the arched bridge.*

*Bottom: The* **Noddy series** *was introduced in 1958, taken from the Enid Blyton television characters. Top:* **Huckleberry Hound**, **Yogi Bear** *and* **Mr Jinks**, *1959-60, Based on the Hanna-Barbera cartoon characters.*

Front: 'Donald Duck' teapot, small size. The remainder of the animals are from the 'Disneys' **Blow-Up** series **Lady and the Tramp** and **Bambi**, dating from 1961-65. The values of these figures varies dramatically with some, **Dachie** for example being very rare. **Thumper, Bambi, Si, Am, Jock, Dachie, Trusty**. Top: **Tramp, Scamp, Lady, Fawn** money bank dating from 1987.

'Bell's Whisky Decanter' commemorating the marriage of HRH Prince Charles and Lady Diana Spencer, 1981. **Bisto Kids**, Boy and Girl salt and pepper shaker, mid 1970s. **Beneagles Scotch Whisky decanter** modelled in the form of a bear, produced between 1981-87. **Toby Jim** Jug. **Sandeman** decanter, produced between 1958-61. **Scottie** teapot, 1953-55, designed by George Lawton, produced with four different tartan decorated lids. **Carrington's Beers** toby jug.

A group of hard paste porcelain animals modelled by 'The famous Faust Lang of Oberammergau . . .' as the advertising by Wade announced, as well as later animal models by Bill Harper. Front: **Baby Polar Bear 'Blow-up'**, 4¼ inches high, **Baby Seal 'Blow-up'** with **Polar Bear 'Blow-up'** above, standing 6 inches high, all three modelled by Bill Harper dating from 1962.

**Stag**, 8¾ inches high, **Polar Bear**, 7¼ inches high and **Panther** 8½ inches high all modelled by Faust Lang in the mid 1930s. In terms of value, Faust Lang models are some of the most sought after and expensive pieces of Wade.

The **World of Survival** series, 1978-82. These animals were manufactured under licence to Survival Anglia Limited after their award winning television series. There were two sets with six animals in each. Due to the high costs involved there were very limited numbers made.

A rare model of **Pogo**, based on the newspaper cartoon strip, produced in 1959 and modelled by William Harper . A slip-cast and unmarked model of a **Cartoon Boy** again by William Harper, 1950s. **Mr Penguin** pepper shaker and **Benny** from the Penguin Family produced in the late 1940s. Mr Penguin can also be found in the same colouring as Benny.

**Dilly** and **Mrs Duck** from the **Quack Quack Family**, designed by Robert Barlow. **Drake** usually marked Wade England in ink and **Seagull**, 1 inch high, made by Wadeheath in the 1940s.

**Mr & Mrs Rabbit**, produced in the late 1940s, 3½ ins high. Two **Angelic figures**, part of three different sets produced from 1959 to through the 1960s. These figures can be found standing, sitting or kneeling and were later added to the bases of candleholders, trays and the like..

A set of **Westminster Piggy Banks**, introduced in 1983.

**Pluto** and one of the **Quinpuplets** dating again from the late 1930s and again rare.

A rare unrecorded underglazed model of **Running Spoof,** hand-written mark A G Fiddes Watt, England in blue. (Courtesy of the Potteries Antique Centre Ltd.)

*An unusual model of a **Seated Deer**, possibly a prototype. The **Big Bad Wolf** musical jug, 1935.*

*A **collection of Gaffer Tetley tableware** made for Lyons Tetley, introduced in 1992. A cruet set, cookie jar and biscuit box.*

***The Thistle and Rose Chess Set**. Designed by Ann Whittet and modelled by Frederick Mellor in 1980, the pieces are based on historical figures of the royal houses dating from the 16th century.*

*A set of four hand-decorated* **Sophisticated Ladies***, although marked My Fair Ladies, 1991-92, by Wade Ceramics Ltd. These did not prove popular, being withdrawn quite quickly.*

*Figure from the two sets of* **My Fair Ladies***, 1990-92, showing some of the various colourways used for these figures.*

*Special commissions made by Wade for G & G Collectables are from left to right and edition size:* **Yogi Bear** *(1500),* **Boo-Boo** *(1500),* **Scoopy Doo** *(2000) and* **Scrappy Doo** *(2000).*

*A set of five graduated elephants, **Treasures**, produced in 1956. Like the Alphabet Train the Elephant Chain was only produced in limited numbers.*

*A **collection of Prototypes**, most slip cast. Many of these figurines were designed by* William Harper.

*Prototype **British Bulldog** made in 1940.*

*On the left is a Wade, Heath & Co. Ltd model of **Mrs Duck** from the Quack Quack nursery ware family made in the 1950s. On the right is a **Studio Szeiler version** made in the 1960s.*

*Old Nanny* an early underglazed seated figure, 1935-39, probably designed by Jessie Van Hallen, *9inches high.*

*Hille Bobbe* by Jessie Van Hallen. *10ins high.*

A set of three graduated **Yacht Wall Plaques**, 1955, made by Wade (Ireland), the largest 4½inches high

**Lucky Leprechauns** made by Wade (Ireland) Ltd between 1956-86. The tallest figure (2¾ inches high) is '**Lucky Leprechaun'** surrounded by '**Little People'** carrying out their various trades.

*Three graduated **McCallum** water jugs. These jugs were produced in mulitcoloured versions and in monochrome. The tallest 6¹/inches high and the smallest 2¹/inches high.*

*A hand painted **Flaxman Ware Wadeheath Wall Plaque**, 1930s, 12¹/inches diameter, with a very well painted scene of a finch on a branch.*

***Dracula** from Nexus/Wade to commemorate the 40th anniversary of Hammer Horror Films*

# Commissions, Event Pieces and Fairs

## Collectors Fair Door Pieces

| Item | Market Value | | Acquired |
|------|-------------|--|----------|
| Owl | £10-£20 | $15-$30 | ☐ |
| Duck | £10-£20 | $15-$30 | ☐ |
| Bear | £10-£20 | $15-$30 | ☐ |

## 21st Century Keepsakes

### Memories Collection

| Item | | Market Value | | Acquired |
|------|--|-------------|--|----------|
| Andy Pandy | 1998 | £50-£70 | $75-$105 | ☐ |
| Looby Loo | 1999 | £40-£60 | $60-$90 | ☐ |
| Bill and Ben | 1999 | £40-£60 | $60-$90 | ☐ |

## UK International Ceramics Ltd

### Flintstones Collection

| Item | | Market Value | | Acquired |
|------|--|-------------|--|----------|
| Fred | 1996 | £40-£60 | $60-$90 | ☐ |
| Wilma | 1996 | £40-£60 | $60-$90 | ☐ |
| Barney | 1997 | £40-£60 | $60-$90 | ☐ |
| Betty | 1997 | £40-£60 | $60-$90 | ☐ |
| Barum Barum | 1998 | £40-£60 | $60-$90 | ☐ |
| Pebbles | 1998 | £40-£60 | $60-$90 | ☐ |

### Felix the Cat

| Item | | Market Value | | Acquired |
|------|--|-------------|--|----------|
| Felix | 1997 | £40-£60 | $60-$90 | ☐ |

### Noddy Set Style 2

| Item | | Market Value | | Acquired |
|------|--|-------------|--|----------|
| Big Ears | 1997 | £40-£60 | $60-$90 | ☐ |
| Noddy | 1997 | £40-£60 | $60-$90 | ☐ |
| Mr Plod | 1999 | £40-£60 | $60-$90 | ☐ |
| Tessie Bear | 1999 | £40-£60 | $60-$90 | ☐ |

### Taurus the Bull

| Item | | | Market Value | | Acquired |
|------|--|--|-------------|--|----------|
| Taurus the Bull | 1999 | 140x180 | £40-£60 | $60-$90 | ☐ |

### Wade Classic Collection

| Item | | Market Value | | Acquired |
|------|--|-------------|--|----------|
| Deer | 1997 | £80-£120 | $120-$185 | ☐ |
| Polar Bear | 1997 | £80-£120 | $120-$185 | ☐ |
| Monkeys | 1997 | £80-£120 | $120-$185 | ☐ |

### Tom and Jerry Style 2

| Item | | Market Value | | Acquired |
|------|--|-------------|--|----------|
| Tom | 1998 | £40-£60 | $60-$90 | ☐ |
| Jerry | 1998 | £40-£60 | $60-$90 | ☐ |

## S&A Collectables Ltd

| Item | | Market Value | | Acquired |
|------|--|-------------|--|----------|
| Jack the Ripper | 1999 | £40-£60 | $60-$90 | ☐ |

## Catkins
### Catkins Collection 1999-2001

| Item | | Market Value | | Acquired |
|---|---|---|---|---|
| Clown | Various colourways | £30-£40 | $45-$60 | ☐ |
| Out for a Duck | White | £30-£40 | $45-$60 | ☐ |
| England Olympic | Blue | £40-£60 | $60-$90 | ☐ |
| Father Christmas | Red | £40-£60 | $60-$90 | ☐ |
| Old Father Time | White | £30-£50 | $45-$75 | ☐ |
| Old Father Time | Grey | £40-£60 | $60-$90 | ☐ |
| Policeman | Blue | £40-£60 | $60-$90 | ☐ |
| Town Crier | Red | £40-£60 | $60-$90 | ☐ |
| Witch | Black | £40-£60 | $60-$90 | ☐ |
| Gypsy | Various colourways | £40-£60 | $60-$90 | ☐ |

## Robert Williamson and Peter Elson
### Gingerbread 1995-1996

| Item | Size (mm) | Market Value | | Acquired |
|---|---|---|---|---|
| Gingerbread Man | 105x80 | £40-£60 | $60-$90 | ☐ |
| Gingerbread Children | 84x84 | £40-£60 | $60-$90 | ☐ |

## Traufler
### Sheep 1992

| Item | | Size (mm) | Market Value | | Acquired |
|---|---|---|---|---|---|
| Large | Cream | 85x145 | £18-£25 | $30-$40 | ☐ |
| Large | Black | 85x145 | £18-£25 | $30-$40 | ☐ |
| Small | Cream | 65x45 | £18-£25 | $30-$40 | ☐ |
| Small | Black | 65x45 | £18-£25 | $30-$40 | ☐ |

### Cockerel Salt Pot and Hen Pepper Pot 1992

| Item | | Size (mm) | Market Value | | Acquired |
|---|---|---|---|---|---|
| Cockerel Salt | White | 110x55 | £18-£25 | $30-$40 | ☐ |
| Cockerel Salt | Yellow | 115x80 | £18-£25 | $30-$40 | ☐ |
| Hen Pepper | White | 90x55 | £18-£25 | $30-$40 | ☐ |
| Hen Pepper | Yellow | 90x70 | £18-£25 | $30-$40 | ☐ |

## St John Ambulance Brigade (UK)
### Bertie Badger

| Item | | Market Value | | Acquired |
|---|---|---|---|---|
| Bertie | 1989 | £120-£180 | $180-$275 | ☐ |
| Money Box | 2001 | £10-£20 | $15-$30 | ☐ |

## Robell Media Promotions Ltd
### Mr Men Collection 1997-1999

| Item | Market Value | | Acquired |
|---|---|---|---|
| Mr Happy | £30-£50 | $45-$75 | ☐ |
| Little Miss Giggles | £30-£50 | $45-$75 | ☐ |
| Mr Bump | £30-£50 | $45-$75 | ☐ |
| Mr Snow | £30-£50 | $45-$75 | ☐ |

## Richleigh Promotions
### Children of the World 1997-1999

| Item | Market Value | | Acquired |
|---|---|---|---|
| Japanese Girl | £30-£50 | $45-$75 | ☐ |
| Japanese Girl | £30-£50 | $45-$75 | ☐ |
| Indian Boy | £30-£50 | $45-$75 | ☐ |
| Spanish Girl | £30-£50 | $45-$75 | ☐ |
| Mexican Boy | £30-£50 | $45-$75 | ☐ |
| Eskimo Girl | £30-£50 | $45-$75 | ☐ |

## Red Rose Tea

### Noahs Ark 2002

| Item | Acquired |
|---|---|
| Bull Elephant | ☐ |
| Cow Elephant | ☐ |
| Ewe | ☐ |
| Ram | ☐ |
| Gander | ☐ |
| Goose | ☐ |
| Hen | ☐ |
| Rooster | ☐ |
| Lion | ☐ |
| Lioness | ☐ |
| Noah | ☐ |
| Noah's Wife | ☐ |
| Rhino Male | ☐ |
| Rhino Female | ☐ |
| Zebra Male | ☐ |
| Zebra Female | ☐ |
| Ark | ☐ |

## Out of the Blue Ceramics

### Superman

| Item | | Market Value | | Acquired |
|---|---|---|---|---|
| Superman | 1998 | £80-£120 | $120-$185 | ☐ |
| Superman | 1998 | £80-£120 | $120-$185 | ☐ |

## Camtrak

| Item | | Market Value | | Acquired |
|---|---|---|---|---|
| Dracula | 1997 | £40-£60 | $60-$90 | ☐ |
| Paddington Bear | | £40-£60 | $60-$90 | ☐ |
| Paddington Bear | Gold Bone | £80-£120 | $120-$185 | ☐ |
| Paddington Bear | Snowy Day | £40-£60 | $60-$90 | ☐ |
| Rupert Bear | 1996 | £40-£60 | $60-$90 | ☐ |
| Rupert Bear | Gold Bone | £150-£200 | $220-$305 | ☐ |
| Dougal | 1995 | £40-£60 | $60-$90 | ☐ |

## West "E" and Scottie

| Item | | Market Value | | Acquired |
|---|---|---|---|---|
| Scottie | 2001 | £20-£30 | $30-$45 | ☐ |
| West "E" | 2001 White | £20-£30 | $30-$45 | ☐ |
| West "E" | 2001 Platinum | Rare | | ☐ |

## Warner Brothers

| Item | | Market Value | | Acquired |
|---|---|---|---|---|
| My Dog Skip | 2001 | £5-£8 | $8-$10 | ☐ |

## Animaland 2001-2002

| Item | Market Value | | Acquired |
|---|---|---|---|
| Baby Bear Cub | £20-£30 | $30-$45 | ☐ |
| Elephant | £20-£30 | $30-$45 | ☐ |
| Mama Otter | £20-£30 | $30-$45 | ☐ |
| Snowy Owl | £20-£30 | $30-$45 | ☐ |

## Pocket Pals

**1999**

| Item | Market Value | | Acquired |
|------|------|------|------|
| Cat Slinky | £8-£12 | $10-$20 | ☐ |
| Hopper | £10-£15 | $15-$25 | ☐ |
| Woofit | £10-£15 | $15-$25 | ☐ |
| Tango | £8-£12 | $10-$20 | ☐ |
| Dog Waggs | £8-£12 | $10-$20 | ☐ |
| Elephant Tusker | £8-£12 | $10-$20 | ☐ |
| Frog Hip Hop | £8-£12 | $10-$20 | ☐ |
| Giraffe Stretch | £8-£12 | $10-$20 | ☐ |
| Hippo Paddles | £8-£12 | $10-$20 | ☐ |
| Mouse Cheesy | £8-£12 | $10-$20 | ☐ |
| Owl Specs | £8-£12 | $10-$20 | ☐ |
| Pig Truffle | £8-£12 | $10-$20 | ☐ |
| Rabbit Bounce | £8-£12 | $10-$20 | ☐ |

## Collect It

**Honey Bear Cub 2000**

| Item | | Market Value | | Acquired |
|------|------|------|------|------|
| Bear Cub | Dark Honey | £3-£5 | $4-$8 | ☐ |
| Bear Cub | Light Honey | £3-£5 | $4-$8 | ☐ |

**Betty Boop – 1997-2000**

| Item | Market Value | | Acquired |
|------|------|------|------|
| Classic Plaque | £70-£100 | $105-$155 | ☐ |
| Liberty Plaque | £70-£100 | $105-$155 | ☐ |

**Fairies – 1998-1999**

| Item | Market Value | | Acquired |
|------|------|------|------|
| Collectania | £30-£50 | $45-$75 | ☐ |
| Collectus | £30-£50 | $45-$75 | ☐ |
| Collectennie | £20-£40 | $30-$60 | ☐ |

## Ceramecca

| Item | | Market Value | | Acquired |
|------|------|------|------|------|
| I'm on my Way | 1999 | £30-£40 | $45-$60 | ☐ |
| Tiny Clanger | 1999 | £40-£60 | $60-$90 | ☐ |
| Sooty | 1998 | £40-£60 | $60-$90 | ☐ |
| Sweep | 1998 | £40-£60 | $60-$90 | ☐ |
| Rupert & Snowman | 1997 | £40-£60 | $60-$90 | ☐ |
| Rupert & Snowman | Gold Buttons | £80-£120 | $120-$185 | ☐ |
| Rupert & Snowman | Pale Blue Scarf | £120-£150 | $180-$230 | ☐ |

**Pokemon – 2001**

| Item | Market Value | | Acquired |
|------|------|------|------|
| Grengar | £8-£12 | $10-$20 | ☐ |
| Jigglypunt | £8-£12 | $10-$20 | ☐ |
| Pikachu | £8-£12 | $10-$20 | ☐ |
| Poliwhirl | £8-£12 | $10-$20 | ☐ |
| Byduck | £8-£12 | $10-$20 | ☐ |

## Key Kollectables

**The Straw Family 1999/2000**

| Item | Market Value | | Acquired |
|------|------|------|------|
| Pa Straw | £30-£50 | $45-$75 | ☐ |
| Ma Straw | £30-£50 | $45-$75 | ☐ |
| Teen Straw | £30-£50 | $45-$75 | ☐ |
| Baby Straw | £30-£50 | $45-$75 | ☐ |

## Trains

### 2001

| Item | | Market Value | | Acquired |
|---|---|---|---|---|
| Spring Train Set | | £30-£40 | $45-$60 | ☐ |
| Spring Train Set | Gold Lettering | £50-£70 | $75-$105 | ☐ |
| Summer Train Set | | £30-£50 | $45-$75 | ☐ |

## K. S. Wader

### Wizard of Oz – 2001

| Item | | Market Value | | Acquired |
|---|---|---|---|---|
| Tin Woodman | Grey | £15-£20 | $20-$30 | ☐ |
| Tin Woodman | White | Rare | | ☐ |

## G&G Collectables

### Hanna Barbera Characters – 1997

| Item | Market Value | | Acquired |
|---|---|---|---|
| Scooby Doo | £40-£60 | $60-$90 | ☐ |
| Scrappy Doo | £40-£60 | $60-$90 | ☐ |
| Mr Jinks | £40-£60 | $60-$90 | ☐ |
| Pixie | £40-£60 | $60-$90 | ☐ |
| Dixie | £40-£60 | $60-$90 | ☐ |
| Boo Boo | £40-£60 | $60-$90 | ☐ |
| Yogi Bear | £40-£60 | $60-$90 | ☐ |
| Huckleberry Hound | £40-£60 | $60-$90 | ☐ |

### Garfield – 1999

| Item | Market Value | | Acquired |
|---|---|---|---|
| Garfield | £50-£70 | $75-$105 | ☐ |

### Characters from Peanuts – 1999-2001

| Item | Market Value | | Acquired |
|---|---|---|---|
| Snoopy & Woodstock | £40-£60 | $60-$90 | ☐ |
| Snoopy hugging Woodstock | £40-£60 | $60-$90 | ☐ |
| Snoopy Happy Holidays | £40-£60 | $60-$90 | ☐ |
| Snoopy Kennel Money Box | £40-£60 | $60-$90 | ☐ |
| Charlie Brown and Linus | £60-£80 | $90-$120 | ☐ |

### Mr Magoo – 1998

| Item | | Market Value | | Acquired |
|---|---|---|---|---|
| Mr Magoo | | £40-£60 | $60-$90 | ☐ |
| Mr Magoo | Gold Bone | Rare | | ☐ |

## Peg and Roger Johnson

### Y2K Pink Elephant

| Item | Market Value | | Acquired |
|---|---|---|---|
| Left Elephant | £10-£20 | $15-$30 | ☐ |
| Right Elephant | £20-£30 | $30-$45 | ☐ |

## E and A Crumpton

### The Long Arm of the Law 1993-1995

| Item | | Market Value | | Acquired |
|---|---|---|---|---|
| The Burglar | | £30-£50 | $45-$75 | ☐ |
| Policeman | Eyes painted | £30-£50 | $45-$75 | ☐ |
| Policeman | | £40-£60 | $60-$90 | ☐ |
| Barrister | | £30-£50 | $45-$75 | ☐ |
| Prisoner | | £30-£50 | $45-$75 | ☐ |

## Cotswold Collectables

**1998-1999**

| Item | | Market Value | | Acquired |
|------|------|------|------|------|
| Tufty | Grey Bone | £40-£60 | $60-$90 | ☐ |
| Tufty | Gold Bone | £50-£70 | $75-$105 | ☐ |

## The Collector

**In the Forest Deep 1997-1999**

| Item | Market Value | | Acquired |
|------|------|------|------|
| Morris Mole | £40-£60 | $60-$90 | ☐ |
| Oswald Owl | £40-£60 | $60-$90 | ☐ |
| Santa | £40-£60 | $60-$90 | ☐ |
| Hedgehog | £40-£60 | $60-$90 | ☐ |
| Bertram Badger | £40-£60 | $60-$90 | ☐ |
| Tailwarmer | £40-£60 | $60-$90 | ☐ |
| Squirrel | £40-£60 | $60-$90 | ☐ |
| Huntsman Fox | £40-£60 | $60-$90 | ☐ |
| Gentleman Rabbit | £40-£60 | $60-$90 | ☐ |

## BJ Promotions

**1999-2000**

| Item | Market Value | | Acquired |
|------|------|------|------|
| Beano Keyring | £8-£12 | $10-$20 | ☐ |
| Dennis | £30-£50 | $45-$75 | ☐ |
| Gnasher | £30-£50 | $45-$75 | ☐ |
| Minnie the Minx | £30-£50 | $45-$75 | ☐ |

## Andy Capp and Flo

**1994-1995**

| Item | Market Value | | Acquired |
|------|------|------|------|
| Andy Capp | £25-£50 | $35-$75 | ☐ |
| Flo | £25-£50 | $35-$75 | ☐ *leo* |

## Blyth Ceramics

**1998-1999**

| Item | | Market Value | | Acquired |
|------|------|------|------|------|
| Sid/Sexist | Grey base | £20-£30 | $30-$45 | ☐ |
| Sid/Sexist | Platinum base | £20-£30 | $30-$45 | ☐ |
| Stan/Fat Slag | Light Grey base | £20-£30 | $30-$45 | ☐ |
| Stan/Fat Slag | Platinum base | £20-£30 | $30-$45 | ☐ |

## Arundel Swap Meets

*Arundel Otter with Pink Salmon*

**1997-2000**

| Item | | Market Value | | Acquired |
|------|------|------|------|------|
| Arundel Duck | 1997, White | £120-£180 | $180-$275 | ☐ |
| Arundel Duck | 1997, Yellow | £40-£60 | $60-$90 | ☐ |
| Arundel Bunny | 1998, Honey | £20-£40 | $30-$60 | ☐ |
| Arundel Bunny | 1998, White | £120-£180 | $180-$275 | ☐ |
| Arundel Teddy Plaque | 1998, Honey | £20-£30 | $30-$45 | ☐ |
| Arundel Chick | 1999, Honey | £20-£30 | $30-$45 | ☐ |

| Item | | Market Value | | Acquired |
|---|---|---|---|---|
| Arundel Chick | 1999, White | £120-£180 | $180-$275 | ☐ |
| Arundel Puppy | 1999, "Steino", White | £20-£30 | $30-$45 | ☐ |
| Arundel Cat | 2000, Honey | £30-£40 | $45-$60 | ☐ |
| Arundel Cat | 2000, White | £60-£100 | $90-$155 | ☐ |
| Arundel Salmon | 2000, Pink | £8-£12 | $10-$20 | ☐ |
| Arundel Clown Singing | 2000, Pearl | £15-£25 | $20-$40 | ☐ |
| Arundel Clown Banjo | 2000, Pearl | £15-£25 | $20-$40 | ☐ |

## Arundel Collectors Meet

**2001**

| Item | | Market Value | | Acquired |
|---|---|---|---|---|
| Arundel Puppy | Honey | £25-£30 | $35-$45 | ☐ |
| Arundel Puppy | White | £70-£100 | $105-$155 | ☐ |
| Clarence the Cow | White | £25-£35 | $35-$55 | ☐ |
| Otter | Grey | £8-£12 | $10-$20 | ☐ |
| Sumo Elephant | Grey | £25-£35 | $35-$55 | ☐ |

## Birmingham Fairs

**1994-1996**

| Item | | Market Value | | Acquired |
|---|---|---|---|---|
| Spaniel | 1994, Honey | £70-£100 | $105-$155 | ☐ |
| Grey Rabbit | 1995, Grey | £60-£90 | $90-$140 | ☐ |
| Smiling Frog | 1996, Green | £40-£60 | $60-$90 | ☐ |

## Collect It Fairs

**1998**

| Item | Market Value | | Acquired |
|---|---|---|---|
| Baby Bear in PJs | £25-£35 | $35-$55 | ☐ |
| Opp's the Bear Style 1 | £30-£40 | $45-$60 | ☐ |
| Travelling Frog | £30-£40 | $45-$60 | ☐ |

## Honey Bunch Bears

**1998**

| Item | | Market Value | | Acquired |
|---|---|---|---|---|
| Bear | Arms up | £20-£30 | $30-$45 | ☐ |
| Bear | Honey Pot | £20-£30 | $30-$45 | ☐ |
| Bear | Honey Pot | £20-£30 | $30-$45 | ☐ |
| Bear | Seated | £20-£30 | $30-$45 | ☐ |
| Bear | Seated | £20-£30 | $30-$45 | ☐ |
| Bear | Sleeping | £20-£30 | $30-$45 | ☐ |

## Dunstable Fairs

**1996-1999**

| Item | | Market Value | | Acquired |
|---|---|---|---|---|
| Timid Mouse | 1996 | £40-£60 | $60-$90 | ☐ |
| Koala Bear | 1997 | £40-£60 | $60-$90 | ☐ |
| Cook Catkins | 1998 | £30-£35 | $45-$55 | ☐ |
| Cook Catkins | 1998 | £40-£60 | $60-$90 | ☐ |
| British Lion | 1999 | £30-£40 | $45-$60 | ☐ |
| British Lion | 1999 | Rare | | ☐ |
| Puppy Love | 1999 | £25-£30 | $35-$45 | ☐ |
| Seals (pair) | 1999 | £25-£30 | $35-$45 | ☐ |
| Shoal of Fish | 1999, Orange, Blue base | £30-£40 | $45-$60 | ☐ |
| Shoal of Fish | 1999 | Rare | | ☐ |

## Stafford Fair

**2000**

| Item | Market Value | | Acquired |
|---|---|---|---|
| Fireman Catkins | £30-£50 | $45-$75 | ☐ |
| Millenium Catkins | £30-£50 | $45-$75 | ☐ |
| Millenium Teddy | £30-£50 | $45-$75 | ☐ |

## Betty Boop 1996-2002

Twenty-one various Betty Boop plaques varying in price from £30/$45 up to £100/$155.

The commissioned pieces, event pieces and miscellaneous have not been fully listed, if you have new pieces that you require information on we advise contacting the Wade Collectors Club.

## Other Commissioneers

| Item | | Market Value | | Acquired |
|---|---|---|---|---|
| Orinoco Womble | 1999 | £40-£60 | $60-$90 | ☐ |
| Thomas the Tank Engine Money Box | 2001 | £30-£50 | $45-$75 | ☐ |
| Frost "E" The Snowman | | £15-£20 | $20-$30 | ☐ |
| Frost "E" The Pearl | | Rare | | ☐ |
| Aran Bear Town Crier | 2001 | £40-£50 | $60-$75 | ☐ |
| Miniature teapots | 2001 | £8-£12 | $10-$20 | ☐ |
| Teddy "E" Bear | | £30-£40 | $45-$60 | ☐ |
| Teddy "E" Bear Gold book | | Rare | | ☐ |
| Santa Claus | 1997 | £30-£40 | $45-$60 | ☐ |
| Little Red Riding Hood | 1998 | £30-£40 | $45-$60 | ☐ |
| Big Bad Wolf | 1999 | £30-£40 | $45-$60 | ☐ |

# Advertising Wares

By far the largest group of wares made by Wade Potteries and the one least recognised by the general public must be their advertising wares. Certainly since the post war period this area has almost been the exclusive domain of the Wade Potteries, initially as a partnership venture under the name 'Wade Regicor' and then running under their own steam as Wade (PDM) Ltd. There can hardly be a public house in Britain or indeed bars on various continents that do not have some Wade ceramics adorning the tables or bar tops. As far as collecting is concerned the wares in this group are not highly sought after by many, although there is a growing core of devoted enthusiasts in countries such as America, Canada and Britain. Within this group the largest number of clients seem to be the breweries and distillers, although others such as Hotel chains, airlines and members of the tobacco industry have placed numerous orders for ashtrays and other promotional items.

The vast majority of advertising related wares have a value under £30-£50/$45-$75 but there are some notable exceptions that have been rapidly increasing in value and are now highly sought after items. The most sought after items in the main are decanters, but of course these would have to have their contents as well as the box to be of greatest value.

## Decanters

**Bell's Old Scotch Whisky.** Since 1988 a special Bell shaped decanter has been produced for United Distillers Bell's whisky every **Christmas** for the UK market and another special design for the South African market. There have also been special issues for royal occasions and commemorating special events. All the decanters have been produced in limited quantities helping to develop the secondary market. In the main the annual UK decanters, produced in green and cream for the first four years then changing to an overall green, are worth between £60-£80/$90-$120, with the exception of 1988 which can be worth between £220-£320/$325-$490. The special decanters for the **South African** market have been produced in the green and cream for the last six years, with designs of '**Curling**', '**Golf**' and '**Fishing**' used between 1992-94 respectively. These appear to be amongst the most collectable , selling for between £300-£400/$445-$610.

Other Bell's decanters such as **Hawaii**, **Wedding** and **Prince Henry** (issued in 1984 to commemorate his birth), boxed and full, are worth between £300-£400/$445-$610, while 'Year of the Sheep' (1991) and 'Year of the Monkey' (1992) are worth between £140-£200/$205-$305. But perhaps the most eagerly sought after of the Bell's decanters, issued in 1981, are the two commemorating **HRH Prince Charles and Lady Diana Spencer**. The full size decanter, issued for £24/$48, is currently selling for between £800-£1200/$1185-$1835, while the mini decanter, 4 inches high, that was issued in a limited edition of between 650 to 700 and presented to the workers of the Bell's distillery, seems to selling for £900-£1200/$1330-$1835.

**Dimple Scotch Whisky** commissioned a series of decanters between 1987 to 1990 – Dragon, Year of the Horse, Year of the Snake, each of which are worth between £400-£500/$590-$765. The Dimple Scotch Whiskey – Coat of Arms is worth £200-£300/$295-$460.

Coach decanter made for **Gordon Chaseton** in a limited edition, 6¹/₂ inches high, £200-£300/$295-$460.

**Thornton & France Sherry Barrel**, 11¹/₄ inches long. Produced in a limited edition of 200 in 1980-81, £150-£200/$220-$305.

The '**John Paul Jones**' US Navy and Marine Corps Ships decanter. First commissioned by Prusser's Ltd in 1983, 8³/₄ inches high. £120-£180/$180-$275. The same shape has been subsequently used on various other decanters.

**British Airways** Liquor Bottle. Modelled in the form of Concorde, 2¹/₄ inches high, £140-£200/$205-$305.

**The English Gentleman's Choice** decanter, 10 inches high, £120-£180/$180-$275.

**Sandeman** decanter. 8¹/₂ inches high. For George G. Sandeman & Co Ltd. 1958-61, £120-£180/$180-$275.

**Baby Chick** spirit decanters. 1961. Made for the Guernsey Cream, Advocaat, Channel Islands Fine Distillers Ltd, Guernsey. Sole Concessionaire Rawlings & Son (London) Ltd. A very limited number of these reached the market, sold through Boots the Chemist, following a fire that destroyed the brewery. £40-£50/$60-$90

**Whitbread Pale Ale Train and Tender**. Produced between February and March 1979 for Whitbread International Belgium. In all only 140 train decanters and 70 tenders were produced, making them highly sought after, the current value being over £1200-£1800/$1775-$2755.

**Beneagles Scotch Whisky**. 4³/₄ inches high. Made by Wade (Ireland) Ltd for Peter Thompson (Perth) Ltd in the form of a brown bear, between 1981-87, £80-£120/$120-$185.

**Cockatoo Spirit container**. 5 inches high, Commissioned by Henry Stratton & Co in 1961, but seems never to have been used for their original purpose, instead being sold through a UK store. It is generally held that there might have been three graduated Cockatoos and three Penguins all made for Henry Stratton & Co. The largest Cockatoo – £120-£180/$180-$275. The largest Penguin – £60-£80/$90-$120.

**Old Parr Tribute** decanter. 7 inches high. 1990-91, £320-£420/$475-$645.

**Black & White Scotch Whisky** decanter, modelled in the form of two Scottie dogs, 7¹/₂ inches high. 1972-1986. £200-£300/$295-$460.

**Findlater's Whisky** decanters commissioned between 1986-1990, one in the shape of a football and the other as a rugby ball, £100-£200/$150-$305.

**The Scotsman** whisky decanter, made for **Asprey & Co** in the 1930s, £300-£400/$445-$610.

**The Irishman** whisky decanter, made for **Asprey & Co** in the 1930s. No price for one of these has been recorded as one has yet to turn up. Unless you know differently??

**Irish Mist** 9 inches high. 1965-66, £80-£120/$120-$185.

**The Potteries** decanter. This decanter was produced in 1994 and 1995, with some 500 decanters (£170-£240/$250-$365) being given to clients and staff at the Glenngoyne Distillery, Drumgoyne, Scotland, in the first year and 350 in 1995. (£130-£180/$190-$275).

## Mugs

**Taunton Cider** have commissioned numerous mugs since 1974, each in a limited edition of 500, the first 50 being numbered, many decorated with a variety of scenes influenced by eighteenth and nineteenth century designs. The most desirable are the larger two handled mugs that are worth between £50-£80/$75-$120.

## Jugs

**Charrington's Beer** toby jug. 7³/₈ inches high. 1960s, £100-£150/$150-$230.

**Toby Jim jug.** 4³/₈ inches high, £60-£80/$90-$120.

**The MacCallum water jug.** A set of three graduated jugs, the tallest 6³/₄ inches (£60-£90/$90-$140) and the smallest 2¹/₄ inches (£40-£60/$60-$90). There was also a **MacCallum ashtray**, 4³/₄ inches diameter (£40-£60/$60-$90).

## Money Banks

| | | |
|---|---|---|
| **Lyon's vintage van** for Lyon's Tetley | | |
| 5¹/₄ inches high | 1990 | £60-£80/$90-$120 |
| **Monster Munch** | | |
| 6¹/₂ inches high | 1987-88 | £80-£100/$120-$155 |
| **Tetley vintage van** for Lyon's Tetley | | |
| 5¹/₄ inches high | 1990 | £50-£70/$75-$105 |
| **'Brew Gaffer'** for Lyon's Tetley | | |
| 5¹/₄ inches high | 1989-90 | £60-£80/$90-$120 |
| **J. W. Thornton Ltd delivery van** | | |
| 4³/₄ inches high | 1993 | £50-£80/$75-$120 |
| **Rington's Tea delivery van** | | |
| 5¹/₄ inches high | | £60-£80/$90-$120 |
| **Boots van** | | |
| 5¹/₄ inches high | | £45-£65/$65-$100 |

**'Sputnik' money box** for MacMillan Davies Brunning Ltd on behalf of the Scarborough Building Society.

| | | |
|---|---|---|
| 4¹/₄ inches high | 1993 | £65-£90/$95-$140 |
| **Harrod's Doorman** | | |
| 6³/₄ inches high | | £60-£80/$90-$120 |
| **'Gaffer'** for Tetley GB Ltd. | | |
| 6 inches high | 1996 | £50-£70/$75-$105 |

**National Westminster Piggy Bank Family**. Produced between 1984-1989 for children under twelve who opened a savings account, each figure being available when six monthly targets had been reached. Once having completed the Piggy Family the account holder was then given a Piggy mug if they joined the National Westminster Bank 100s club. In order of qualification the mugs were:

| | | |
|---|---|---|
| **Woody** | 5 inches high | £20-£30/$30-$45 |
| **Annabel** | 6³/₈ inches high | £30-£40/$45-$60 |
| **Maxwell** | 6³/₄ inches high | £50-£80/$75-$120 |
| **Lady Hillary** | 7 inches high | £40-£60/$60-$90 |
| **Sir Nathaniel** | 7¹/₄ inches high | £50-£70/$75-$105 |

**Jim Beam van money box**. 5¼ inches high. Produced in two different colourways for the 26th Annual Convention, Seattle, Washington, July, 1996, in a limited edition of 305, £80-£120/$120-$185.

## Miscellaneous

**'Pex' Fairy**. Made for Pex Stockings by Wade (Ulster) Ltd. 2⅜ inches high. 1948-50. This figure is very rare and seems to have been produced in various colourways as well as being incorporated onto a base as a candleholder. The candleholder is generally of higher value, £400-£600/$590-$920.

**Guinness Promotional Figures**. Made in 1968/9 these figures were produced in a limited number and are therefore very sought after.

| | | |
|---|---|---|
| **Tony Weller** | 3 inches high | £120-£180/$180-$275 |
| **Tweedle Dee & Tweedle Dum** | 2⅞ inches high | £140-£200/$205-$305 |
| **Wellington Boot** | 3½ inches high | £120-£180/$180-$275 |
| **Mad Hatter** | 3¼ inches high | £140-£200/$205-$305 |
| **Tetley Van Tea Caddy** 1994-95 | 5⅜ inches high | £80-£120/$120-$185 |
| **The Brewmaster,** made for Flowers Beer 1960s | 5¼ inches high | £200-£300/$295-$460 |

**Robertson's Gollies 'Bandstand' figures**. Commissioned in the early 1960s the set contains seven figures, such as the Saxophone player, Trumpet Player, Drummer, etc., each of which are currently worth between £150-£200/$220-$305. These figures, which in this case should have white bases, were reproduced later by another company with black bases. The Wade Golly musician were displayed on a simple white circular bandstand.

**Hamm's Bear 'Santa's Helper'**. Commissioned by Silver State Specialities in 1995 and 1996 in limited editions, £30-£50/$45-$75.

**Whitbread Pin Badge and Ceramic Frog**. Only a few thousand of these were made, the frog being attached to the metal badge with double sided tape. The badge – 2½ inches diameter. The frog – 1½ inches long. 1987. The value lies in both items being together., £30-£40/$45-$60.

# Price Guide

# Animals

From the late 1920s George Wade produced cellulose-finished animal figures of medium size. In a similar fashion to the celluose figurines, these lost their popularity due to the unstable nature of the cellulose and were replaced in the early 1930s with a line of slip cast, porcelain figure with an underglaze finish, and if applied carried the mark of number 4, seen in the Marks and Backstamps section. 1935 saw George Wade introduce a range that consisted of new models as well as some using the cellulose moulds. The new mould animals were based on wood carvings by Faust Lang, were of extremely high qualityand so expensive, and production was only stopped due to the outbreak of war in 1939. These models carry the 'Wade England' backstamp along with the name of the figure and occasionally year of manufacture. The factory produced a set of bird figures, also based on Lang designs, but due to the lateness of their introduction they weren't marketed fully until after the war, when Wade Heath obtained the moulds and produced them until the mid 1950s.

Wade Heath produced a set of oranmental comical animal figures from the late 1930s until, again war stopped production and there is no record that these were continued once hostilities ceased. After the war Wade Heath obtained some moulds from George Wade and along with some of their own moulds produced a range of animal figures until the mid 1950s.

## Abbreviations in price guide

E = Early   L = Late   M = Mid

| Name | Size | Production | Market Price | | Acquired |
|------|------|-----------|-------------|---|----------|
| **Bears** | | | | | |
| Bear | $1\frac{5}{8}$x$2\frac{1}{2}$ | 1930-1939 | £250-£350 | $370-$535 | ☐ |
| Brown Bear (F. Lang) | $9\frac{1}{2}$ | 1939 | £900-£1500 | $1330-$2295 | ☐ |
| Polar Bear (F. Lang) | $7\frac{1}{4}$ | 1935-1939 | £1500-£2000 | $2220-$3060 | ☐ |
| Polar Bear (Ireland) | | 1978-1980 | £500-£700 | $740-$1070 | ☐ |
| Koala Bear (Ireland) | 7 | 1978-1980 | £500-£800 | $740-$1225 | ☐ |
| **Bears (Panda)** | | | | | |
| Baby Panda | $1\frac{1}{2}$x$2\frac{1}{4}$ | 1930-1939 | £200-£300 | $295-$460 | ☐ |
| Giant Panda (F. Lang) | $7\frac{1}{2}$ | 1939 | £900-£1200 | $1330-$1835 | ☐ |
| **Birds** | | | | | |
| Budgerigar (F. Lang) | $6\frac{3}{4}$ | 1935-1939 | £500-£700 | $740-$1070 | ☐ |
| Budgerigar (F. Lang) | 8 | L30s-M50s | £500-£700 | $740-$1070 | ☐ |
| Cheeky Duckling | | 1937-1939 | £140-£180 | $205-$275 | ☐ |
| Chick | $1\frac{3}{4}$ | 1930-1939 | £120-£180 | $180-$275 | ☐ |
| Cockatoo (F. Lang) | $5\frac{3}{4}$ | 1935-1939 | £500-£700 | $740-$1070 | ☐ |
| Cockatoo (F. Lang) | 6 | L30s-M50s | £500-£700 | $740-$1070 | ☐ |
| Drake and Daddy | $3\frac{1}{8}$x2 | 1930-1939 | £140-£180 | $205-$275 | ☐ |
| Drake and Daddy | $3\frac{1}{8}$x2 | 1948-1959 | £120-£180 | $180-$275 | ☐ |
| Duck | $1\frac{5}{8}$x$1\frac{3}{4}$ | 1930-1939 | £120-£180 | $180-$275 | ☐ |
| Duck | $1\frac{1}{2}$x$1\frac{1}{4}$ | 1930-1939 | £120-£180 | $180-$275 | ☐ |

| Name | Size | Production | Market Price | | Acquired |
|------|------|-----------|--------------|--|----------|
| Duck | $1\frac{1}{2}\times1\frac{3}{4}$ | 1930-1939 | £120-£180 | $180-$275 | ☐ |
| Duck | $2\frac{3}{4}\times2\frac{1}{8}$ | 1930-1939 | £120-£180 | $180-$275 | ☐ |
| Duck | $1\frac{3}{4}\times3\frac{1}{8}$ | 1930-1939 | £120-£180 | $180-$275 | ☐ |
| Duck | $3\times3\frac{1}{8}$ | 1930-1939 | £120-£180 | $180-$275 | ☐ |
| Duck | $3\times2\frac{1}{8}$ | 1930-1939 | £120-£180 | $180-$275 | ☐ |
| Duck | $2\times\frac{7}{8}$ | 1930-1939 | £120-£180 | $180-$275 | ☐ |
| (Long Necked - Head up) | | | | | |
| Duck | $2\times\frac{3}{4}$ | 1930-1939 | £120-£180 | $180-$275 | ☐ |
| (Long Necked – Head down) | | | | | |
| Duck | $2\times\frac{3}{4}$ | 1948-1959 | £120-£180 | $180-$275 | ☐ |
| (Long Necked – Head down) | | | | | |
| Duck | $2\times\frac{7}{8}$ | 1948-1959 | £120-£180 | $180-$275 | ☐ |
| (Long Necked – Head up) | | | | | |
| Goldfinch (Head down) | 4 | L30s-M50s | £200-£300 | $295-$460 | ☐ |
| Goldfinch (Head up) | 4 | L30s-M50s | £200-£300 | $295-$460 | ☐ |
| Grebe (F. Lang) | $9\frac{1}{4}$ | 1935-1939 | £700-£1000 | $1035-$1530 | ☐ |
| Hawk | $13\frac{1}{2}$ | Post-war | (not available) | | ☐ |
| Heron (F. Lang) | 7 | L30s-M50s | £800-£1200 | $1185-$1835 | ☐ |
| Long Necked Duck | $3\frac{3}{4}\times1\frac{3}{8}$ | 1930-1939 | £250-£350 | $370-$535 | ☐ |
| Mallard | $3\frac{5}{8}\times3\frac{1}{2}$ | 1930-1939 | £250-£350 | $370-$535 | ☐ |
| Owl | $5\frac{1}{2}$ | c1940 | £500-£700 | $740-$1035 | ☐ |
| Parrot (F. Lang) | $10\frac{1}{4}$ | 1935-1939 | £1200-£1800 | $1775-$2775 | ☐ |
| Pelican | 5 | L30s-M50s | £250-£300 | $370-$460 | ☐ |
| Seagull | 1 | 1948-1959 | £120-£180 | $180-$275 | ☐ |
| Toucan | | 1930s | £200-£300 | $295-$460 | ☐ |
| Two Budgerigars (F. Lang) | $7\frac{3}{4}$ | 1935-1939 | £800-£1200 | $1185-$1835 | ☐ |
| Woodpecker (F. Lang) | 6 | L30s-M50s | £500-£700 | $740-$1035 | ☐ |
| **Birds (Connoisseurs Collection)** | | | | | |
| Bullfinch | $7\frac{1}{4}$ | 1978-1982 | £250-£350 | $370-$535 | ☐ |
| Coal Tit | $5\frac{3}{4}$ | 1978-1982 | £250-£350 | $370-$535 | ☐ |
| Goldcrest | $5\frac{1}{4}$ | 1978-1982 | £250-£350 | $370-$535 | ☐ |
| Nuthatch | $5\frac{1}{2}$ | 1978-1982 | £250-£350 | $370-$535 | ☐ |
| Robin | 5 | 1978-1982 | £250-£350 | $370-$535 | ☐ |
| Wren | $4\frac{1}{2}$ | 1978-1982 | £250-£350 | $370-$535 | ☐ |
| Bearded Tit | $6\frac{1}{2}$ | 1980-1982 | £250-£350 | $370-$535 | ☐ |
| Dipper | $5\frac{1}{2}$ | 1980-1982 | £250-£350 | $370-$535 | ☐ |
| Kingfisher | 7 | 1980-1982 | £250-£350 | $370-$535 | ☐ |
| Redstart | 7 | 1980-1982 | £250-£350 | $370-$535 | ☐ |
| Woodpecker | $6\frac{1}{2}$ | 1980-1982 | £250-£350 | $370-$535 | ☐ |
| Yellow Wagtail | $4\frac{1}{2}$ | 1980-1982 | £250-£350 | $370-$535 | ☐ |
| **Ducks (Quack Quack Family)** | | | | | |
| Dack | $1\frac{1}{2}\times1\frac{1}{8}$ | 1948-1959 | £150-£200 | $220-$305 | ☐ |
| Dilly | $1\frac{1}{2}\times1\frac{1}{8}$ | 1948-1959 | £150-£200 | $220-$305 | ☐ |
| Mr Duck | $2\frac{1}{2}\times1\frac{1}{2}$ | 1948-1959 | £150-£200 | $220-$305 | ☐ |
| Mrs Duck | $2\frac{1}{2}\times1\frac{1}{2}$ | 1948-1959 | £150-£200 | $220-$305 | ☐ |
| **Camels** | | | | | |
| Camel (F Lang?) | $7\frac{3}{4}\times6\frac{3}{4}$ | 1935-1939 | £800-£1200 | $1185-$1835 | ☐ |
| **Cats** | | | | | |
| Cat | $1\frac{1}{2}\times2\frac{1}{8}$ | 1930-1939 | £80-£120 | $120-$185 | ☐ |
| Cat | $1\frac{1}{8}\times2\frac{7}{8}$ | 1930-1939 | £80-£120 | $120-$185 | ☐ |
| Cat | $1\frac{1}{4}\times1\frac{3}{4}$ | 1930-1939 | £80-£120 | $120-$185 | ☐ |

| Name | Size | Production | Market Price | | Acquired |
|---|---|---|---|---|---|
| Cat | $1\frac{1}{2}$x$2\frac{1}{8}$ | 1930-1939 | £80-£120 | $120-$185 | ☐ |
| Cat | 1x$2\frac{3}{4}$ | 1930-1939 | £80-£120 | $120-$185 | ☐ |
| Cat | 1x$2\frac{3}{4}$ | 1930-1939 | £80-£120 | $120-$185 | ☐ |
| Cat | $1\frac{1}{2}$ | 1948-1959 | £70-£100 | $105-$155 | ☐ |
| Cat | $1\frac{1}{2}$ | 1948-1959 | £70-£100 | $105-$155 | ☐ |
| Cat | $1\frac{1}{2}$ | 1948-1959 | £70-£100 | $105-$155 | ☐ |
| Cat | $1\frac{1}{2}$ | 1948-1959 | £70-£100 | $105-$155 | ☐ |
| Cat | $1\frac{1}{2}$ | 1948-1959 | £70-£100 | $105-$155 | ☐ |
| **Cows** | | | | | |
| Calf | $2\frac{3}{8}$x$1\frac{1}{4}$ | 1930-1939 | £220-£300 | $325-$460 | ☐ |
| **Deers** | | | | | |
| Deer | $1\frac{1}{8}$x$1\frac{1}{4}$ | 1930-1939 | £150-£180 | $220-$275 | ☐ |
| Deer | $2\frac{1}{2}$x$1\frac{3}{4}$ | 1930-1939 | £140-£180 | $205-$275 | ☐ |
| Stag | $8\frac{3}{4}$ | 1935-1939 | £800-£1200 | $1185-$1835 | ☐ |
| **Dogs** | | | | | |
| Airedale | 7x8 | 1927-1937 | £200-£300 | $295-$460 | ☐ |
| Alsatian | $10\frac{1}{4}$x18 | 1927-1937 | £150-£200 | $220-$305 | ☐ |
| Alsatian | $4\frac{3}{4}$x$8\frac{3}{4}$ | 1927-1937 | £200-£300 | $295-$460 | ☐ |
| Begging Puppy | $3\frac{1}{8}$x$1\frac{3}{4}$ | 1930-1939 | £150-£200 | $220-$305 | ☐ |
| Borzoi | 12x$12\frac{1}{2}$ | 1927-1937 | £700-£1000 | $1035-$1530 | ☐ |
| Dachshund | $3\frac{1}{8}$x$1\frac{1}{2}$ | 1930-1939 | £200-£300 | $295-$460 | ☐ |
| Dalmation | $8\frac{3}{4}$x$12\frac{1}{2}$ | 1927-1937 | £500-£1800 | $740-$2775 | ☐ |
| Pongo | $5\frac{5}{8}$x$5\frac{1}{8}$ | 1937-1939 | £100-£150 | $150-$230 | ☐ |
| Pongo | $5\frac{1}{8}$x$4\frac{5}{8}$ | 1937-1939 | £80-£120 | $120-$185 | ☐ |
| Pongo | $4\frac{5}{8}$x4 | 1937-1939 | £50-£70 | $75-$105 | ☐ |
| Scottie | $4\frac{3}{4}$x$6\frac{1}{4}$ | 1927-1937 | £220-£300 | $325-$460 | ☐ |
| Setter | 6x$9\frac{3}{4}$ | 1927-1937 | £220-£300 | $325-$460 | ☐ |
| Setter | $3\frac{1}{2}$x$2\frac{1}{4}$ | 1930-1939 | £150-£200 | $220-$305 | ☐ |
| Setter | $3\frac{1}{2}$ | 1948-1959 | £150-£200 | $220-$305 | ☐ |
| Sitting Scottie | | 1937-1939 | £70-£100 | $105-$155 | ☐ |
| Spaniel | $5\frac{1}{2}$x5 | 1927-1937 | £300-£400 | $445-$660 | ☐ |
| Spaniel (Playful Puppy) | $2\frac{1}{2}$x$5\frac{1}{2}$ | 1927-1937 | £250-£300 | $370-$460 | ☐ |
| Terrier | 7x8 | 1927-1937 | £300-£400 | $445-$610 | ☐ |
| Terrier | | 1937-1939 | £70-£100 | $105-$155 | ☐ |
| Walking Scottie | | 1937-1939 | £90-£130 | $135-$200 | ☐ |
| **Dogs (Championship Dogs)** | | | | | |
| Afghan Hound | 3x$3\frac{3}{8}$ | 1975-1981 | £40-£60 | $60-$90 | ☐ |
| Cocker Spaniel | $2\frac{7}{8}$x$3\frac{5}{8}$ | 1975-1981 | £50-£80 | $75-$120 | ☐ |
| Collie | $3\frac{1}{8}$x4 | 1975-1981 | £50-£80 | $75-$120 | ☐ |
| English Setter | $2\frac{3}{4}$x$4\frac{1}{8}$ | 1975-1981 | £50-£80 | $75-$120 | ☐ |
| Old English Sheepdog | $3\frac{1}{8}$x3 | 1975-1981 | £50-£80 | $75-$120 | ☐ |
| **Dogs and Puppies** | | | | | |
| Alsatian (Adult) | $2\frac{1}{2}$x$2\frac{3}{8}$ | 1969-1982 | £8-£12 | $10-$20 | ☐ |
| Alsatian (Puppy) | $1\frac{1}{4}$x2 | 1969-1982 | £8-£12 | $10-$20 | ☐ |
| Alsatian (Puppy) | $1\frac{3}{4}$x$1\frac{5}{8}$ | 1969-1982 | £8-£12 | $10-$20 | ☐ |
| Cairn (Adult) | $2\frac{1}{2}$x$2\frac{3}{4}$ | 1969-1982 | £8-£12 | $10-$20 | ☐ |
| Cairn (Puppy) | $1\frac{1}{2}$x$1\frac{3}{8}$ | 1969-1982 | £8-£12 | $10-$20 | ☐ |
| Cairn (Puppy) | $1\frac{3}{8}$x2 | 1969-1982 | £8-£12 | $10-$20 | ☐ |
| Corgi (Adult) | $2\frac{1}{4}$x$2\frac{1}{4}$ | 1979-1982 | £15-£25 | $20-$40 | ☐ |
| Corgi (Puppy) | $1\frac{5}{8}$x$1\frac{3}{8}$ | 1979-1982 | £10-£20 | $15-$30 | ☐ |
| Corgi (Puppy) | $1\frac{1}{8}$ | 1979-1982 | £10-£20 | $15-$30 | ☐ |

| Name | Size | Production | Market Price | | Acquired |
|------|------|-----------|-------------|---|----------|
| Red Setter (Adult) | $2^{1}/_{4}$x$2^{7}/_{8}$ | 1979-1982 | £8-£12 | $10-$20 | ☐ |
| Red Setter (Puppy) | $1^{1}/_{2}$x$1^{3}/_{4}$ | 1979-1982 | £8-£12 | $10-$20 | ☐ |
| Red Setter (Puppy) | $1^{1}/_{2}$x$1^{3}/_{4}$ | 1979-1982 | £8-£12 | $10-$20 | ☐ |
| Yorkshire Terrier (Adult) | $2^{1}/_{8}$x$1^{5}/_{8}$ | 1979-1982 | £20-£40 | $30-$60 | ☐ |
| Yorkshire Terrier (Puppy) | $1^{3}/_{8}$x$1^{1}/_{2}$ | 1979-1982 | £15-£25 | $20-$40 | ☐ |
| Yorkshire Terrier (Puppy) | $1^{1}/_{2}$x$1^{1}/_{4}$ | 1979-1982 | £15-£25 | $20-$40 | ☐ |
| **Donkeys** | | | | | |
| Cheerful Charlie | $4^{3}/_{8}$x$2^{1}/_{8}$ | 1948-1959 | £150-£200 | $220-$305 | ☐ |
| Doleful Dan | $4^{3}/_{8}$x$2^{1}/_{8}$ | 1948-1959 | £150-£200 | $220-$305 | ☐ |
| Donkey | $1^{7}/_{8}$x$1^{1}/_{2}$ | 1930-1939 | £150-£200 | $220-$305 | ☐ |
| Foal | $1^{1}/_{2}$x$1^{1}/_{4}$ | 1930-1939 | £150-£200 | $220-$305 | ☐ |
| **Elephants** | | | | | |
| Elephant | $2$x$2^{1}/_{2}$ | 1930-1939 | £180-£240 | $265-$365 | ☐ |
| Elephant | 2 | 1948-1959 | £120-£180 | $180-$275 | ☐ |
| Elephant (Ireland) | | 1978-1980 | £400-£600 | $590-$920 | ☐ |
| Jumbo Jim | | 1937-1939 | £120-£180 | $180-$275 | ☐ |
| **Ermines** | | | | | |
| Ermine (F. Lang) | $9^{1}/_{2}$x3 | 1935-1939 | £1700-£2400 | $2515-$3670 | ☐ |
| **Frog Family - Style 1 Green** | | | | | |
| Mr Frog | 40x58 | 1948-1952 | £100-£150 | $150-$230 | ☐ |
| Mrs Frog | 40x58 | 1948-1952 | £100-£150 | $150-$230 | ☐ |
| Boy Frog | 28x38 | 1948-1952 | £100-£150 | $150-$230 | ☐ |
| Girl Frog | 28x38 | 1948-1952 | £100-£150 | $150-$230 | ☐ |
| **Giraffes** | | | | | |
| Giraffe (F. Lang) | 3x4 | 1935-1939 | £400-£600 | $590-$920 | ☐ |
| **Goats** | | | | | |
| Chamois Kid | $5^{1}/_{4}$x$3^{1}/_{4}$ | 1935-1939 | £500-£700 | $740-$1035 | ☐ |
| Ibex | $2^{1}/_{4}$x$2^{1}/_{4}$ | 1930-1939 | £250-£300 | $370-$460 | ☐ |
| **Horse Set** | | | | | |
| Foal | $1^{7}/_{8}$x2 | 1974-1978 | £10-£15 | $15-$20 | ☐ |
| Foal | $1^{3}/_{8}$x2 | 1974-1978 | £10-£15 | $15-$20 | ☐ |
| Horse | $2^{3}/_{4}$x3 | 1974-1978 | £10-£15 | $15-$20 | ☐ |
| Foal | $1^{1}/_{2}$x$1^{7}/_{8}$ | 1978-1981 | £35-£45 | $50-$70 | ☐ |
| Foal | $1^{1}/_{4}$x$1^{7}/_{8}$ | 1978-1981 | £35-£45 | $50-$70 | ☐ |
| Horse | $2^{1}/_{2}$x$2^{3}/_{4}$ | 1978-1981 | £35-£45 | $50-$70 | ☐ |
| **Horses** | | | | | |
| Dartmoor Pony | $4^{7}/_{8}$x$4^{1}/_{4}$ | 1935-1939 | £250-£300 | $370-$460 | ☐ |
| Dartmoor Pony | 4x4 | 1935-1939 | £250-£300 | $370-$460 | ☐ |
| Foal | $2^{1}/_{2}$x$2^{1}/_{2}$ | 1930-1939 | £180-£240 | $265-$365 | ☐ |
| Foal | $2$x$2^{1}/_{4}$ | 1930-1939 | £180-£240 | $265-$365 | ☐ |
| Horse | $7^{3}/_{4}$x$6^{3}/_{4}$ | 1935-1939 | £600-£800 | $890-$1225 | ☐ |
| **Hippopotamus** | | | | | |
| Hippopotamus | $1^{3}/_{8}$x$4^{1}/_{2}$ | 1930s | £400-£600 | $590-$920 | ☐ |
| **Lions** | | | | | |
| Lion Cub | | | | | |
| – Paw down (F. Lang) | $5^{1}/_{4}$x$7^{1}/_{4}$ | 1935-1939 | £1700-£2400 | $2515-$3670 | ☐ |
| – Paw up (F. Lang) | $5^{1}/_{4}$x$7^{1}/_{4}$ | 1935-1939 | £1700-£2400 | $2515-$3670 | ☐ |
| Lion (Ireland) | | 1978-1980 | £400-£600 | $590-$920 | ☐ |
| **Monkeys** | | | | | |
| Capuchin (F. Lang) | 10 | 1935-1939 | £1000-£1500 | $1480-$2295 | ☐ |
| Monkey | $1^{1}/_{8}$x$3^{3}/_{4}$ | 1930-1939 | £180-£240 | $265-$365 | ☐ |

| Name | Size | Production | Market Price | | Acquired |
|------|------|-----------|--------------|---|----------|
| Monkey | $2\frac{1}{2}$x2 | 1930-1939 | £280-£300 | $415-$460 | ☐ |
| **Otters** | | | | | |
| Otter (F. Lang) | 4x10$\frac{3}{4}$ | 1935-1939 | £1000-£1500 | $1480-$2295 | ☐ |
| **Panthers** | | | | | |
| Panther (F. Lang) | 8x5 | 1935-1939 | £700-£1000 | $1035-$1530 | ☐ |
| **Penguin Family** | | | | | |
| Benny | 2x1 | 1948-1959 | £100-£150 | $150-$230 | ☐ |
| Mr Penguin | $3\frac{1}{2}$x1$\frac{1}{2}$ | 1948-1959 | £100-£150 | $150-$230 | ☐ |
| Mrs Penguin | 3x1$\frac{1}{2}$ | 1948-1959 | £100-£150 | $150-$230 | ☐ |
| Penny | 2x1 | 1948-1959 | £100-£150 | $150-$230 | ☐ |
| **Penguins** | | | | | |
| Penguin | $2\frac{3}{4}$x2$\frac{1}{4}$ | 1930-1939 | £180-£200 | $265-$305 | ☐ |
| **Pig Family** | | | | | |
| Boy Pig | | | Rare | | ☐ |
| Girl Pig | | | Rare | | ☐ |
| Mr Pig | | | £70-£90 | $105-$140 | ☐ |
| Mrs Pig | | | £70-£90 | $105-$140 | ☐ |
| **Rabbit Family** | | | | | |
| Fluff | $1\frac{1}{2}$x1$\frac{1}{8}$ | 1948-1959 | £100-£150 | $150-$230 | ☐ |
| Mr Rabbit | $3\frac{1}{2}$x1$\frac{1}{2}$ | 1948-1959 | £100-£150 | $150-$230 | ☐ |
| Mrs Rabbit | $3\frac{1}{2}$x1$\frac{1}{2}$ | 1948-1959 | £100-£150 | $150-$230 | ☐ |
| Puff | $1\frac{1}{2}$x1$\frac{1}{8}$ | 1948-1959 | £100-£150 | $150-$230 | ☐ |
| **Rabbits** | | | | | |
| Bunny | $\frac{7}{8}$x1$\frac{1}{8}$ | 1930-1939 | £40-£60 | $60-$90 | ☐ |
| Bunny | $\frac{7}{8}$x1 | 1948-1959 | £40-£60 | $60-$90 | ☐ |
| Crouching Rabbit | | 1937-1939 | £100-£150 | $150-$230 | ☐ |
| Double Bunnies | $\frac{7}{8}$x1 | 1930-1939 | £80-£120 | $120-$185 | ☐ |
| Double Bunnies | $1\frac{1}{4}$x1$\frac{3}{4}$ | 1930-1939 | £80-£120 | $120-$185 | ☐ |
| Double Bunnies | $1\frac{5}{8}$x2$\frac{3}{4}$ | 1930-1939 | £80-£120 | $120-$185 | ☐ |
| Double Bunnies | $\frac{7}{8}$ | 1948-1959 | £80-£120 | $120-$185 | ☐ |
| Double Bunnies | $1\frac{5}{8}$x1 | 1948-1959 | £80-£120 | $120-$185 | ☐ |
| Kissing Bunnies | $2\frac{1}{2}$x2$\frac{3}{4}$ | 1930-1939 | £80-£120 | $120-$185 | ☐ |
| Kissing Bunnies | $2\frac{1}{2}$x2$\frac{3}{4}$ | 1948-1959 | £80-£120 | $120-$185 | ☐ |
| Laughing Rabbit | $5\frac{5}{8}$x$\frac{5}{8}$ | 1937-1939 | £60-£100 | $90-$155 | ☐ |
| Laughing Rabbit | $6\frac{3}{8}$x2$\frac{7}{8}$ | 1937-1939 | £60-£100 | $90-$155 | ☐ |
| Laughing Rabbit | 7x3 | 1937-1939 | £60-£100 | $90-$155 | ☐ |
| Little Laughing Bunny | $2\frac{1}{2}$x1$\frac{1}{2}$ | L40s-E50s | | | ☐ |
| Old Buck | $6\frac{5}{8}$x5$\frac{1}{8}$ | 1937-1939 | £200-£300 | $295-$460 | ☐ |
| Rabbit (miniature) | | 1937-1939 | £60-£80 | $90-$120 | ☐ |
| Rabbit (small) | | 1937-1939 | £70-£100 | $105-$155 | ☐ |
| Rabbit (medium) | | 1937-1939 | £80-£120 | $120-$185 | ☐ |
| Rabbit (large) | | 1937-1939 | £120-£180 | $180-$275 | ☐ |
| Standing Rabbit | $2\frac{5}{8}$x1$\frac{3}{8}$ | 1930-1939 | £70-£100 | $105-$155 | ☐ |
| Standing Rabbit | $2\frac{1}{2}$ | 1948-1959 | £70-£100 | $105-$155 | ☐ |
| **Razorback** | | | | | |
| Razorback | 5x8 | | £700-£1000 | $1035-$1530 | ☐ |
| **Rhinoceros** | | | | | |
| Rhino (Ireland) | | 1978-1980 | £400-£600 | $590-$920 | ☐ |
| Rhinoceros Ashtray | $8\frac{1}{4}$ | 1962 | £300-£400 | $445-$610 | ☐ |
| Rhinoceros Ashtray | $5\frac{1}{2}$ | 1962 | £300-£400 | $445-$610 | ☐ |
| **Sealions** | | | | | |

| Name | Size | Production | Market Price | | Acquired |
|---|---|---|---|---|---|
| Sealion | | 1960 | £150-£200 | $220-$305 | ☐ |
| **Sheep** | | | | | |
| Lamb | 2⅛x2 | 1930-1939 | £120-£180 | $180-$275 | ☐ |
| Lamb | 2x2⅜ | 1930-1939 | £120-£180 | $180-$275 | ☐ |
| Lamb | 2x2⅜ | 1930-1939 | £120-£180 | $180-$275 | ☐ |
| Lamb | 1½x1¼ | 1930-1939 | £120-£180 | $180-$275 | ☐ |
| Lamb | 2x2⅜ | 1948-1959 | £120-£180 | $180-$275 | ☐ |
| Lamb | 2 | 1948-1959 | £120-£180 | $180-$275 | ☐ |
| **Squirrels** | | | | | |
| Squirrel | 1½ | 1948-1959 | £70-£90 | $105-$140 | ☐ |
| Squirrel | 1⅝x2⅛ | 1930-1939 | £80-£120 | $120-$185 | ☐ |
| Squirrel | 2½x2½ | 1930-1939 | £150-£180 | $220-$275 | ☐ |
| Squirrel | | 1937-1939 | £150-£180 | $220-$275 | ☐ |
| **Survival** | | 1991 | £3000-£4000 | $4440-$6120 | ☐ |
| **Tortoise Family** | | | | | |
| 'Slow Fe' Baby Tortoise | 1¼x3 | 1969-1970 | £50-£80 | $75-$120 | ☐ |
| Baby Tortoise | 1¼x3 | 1960 | £15-£20 | $20-$30 | ☐ |
| Baby Tortoise | ⅞x2 | 1960 | £15-£20 | $20-$30 | ☐ |
| Extra Large Tortoise | 2⅜x6 | 1973 | £60-£80 | $90-$120 | ☐ |
| Large Tortoise | 2¾x4 | 1958 | £25-£30 | $35-$45 | ☐ |
| Tortoise | 1¼x3 | 1930s | £400-£600 | $590-$920 | ☐ |
| **Walrus** | | | | | |
| Walrus (Ireland) | 6 | 1978-1980 | £400-£600 | $590-$920 | ☐ |
| **World of Survival** | | | | | |
| African Elephant | 6x10 | 1978-1982 | £300-£400 | $445-$610 | ☐ |
| African Lion | 4½x8 | 1978-1982 | £200-£400 | $295-$660 | ☐ |
| American Bison | 4½x8 | 1978-1982 | £200-£300 | $295-$460 | ☐ |
| Black Rhinoceros | 4½x9½ | 1978-1982 | £300-£400 | $445-$610 | ☐ |
| Polar Bear | 4½x8½ | 1978-1982 | £250-£300 | $370-$460 | ☐ |
| Tiger | 3½x8 | 1978-1982 | £200-£300 | $295-$460 | ☐ |
| African (Cape) Buffalo | 5x9¼ | 1980-1982 | £600-£700 | $890-$1070 | ☐ |
| American Brown Bear | 4x5½ | 1980-1982 | £200-£300 | $295-$460 | ☐ |
| American Cougar (Puma) | 4x9 | 1980-1982 | £300-£400 | $445-$610 | ☐ |
| Gorilla | 5½x5¾ | 1980-1982 | £300-£400 | $445-$610 | ☐ |
| Harp Seal & Pup | 3¾x9 | 1980-1982 | £600-£700 | $890-$1070 | ☐ |
| Hippopotamus | 4½x10 | 1980-1982 | £300-£400 | $445-$610 | ☐ |

# Aquarium

This consists of a set of six models and were commissioned from George Wade by King British Aquarium Accessories Ltd. Equal number of each model was produced over a three to four year production period. The Seahorse and the Snail are the most difficult to find.

| Name | Size | Production | Market Price | | Acquired |
|---|---|---|---|---|---|
| Bridge | 2¾x3⅝ | 1974-1990 | £70-£90 | $105-$140 | ☐ |
| Diver | 2¾x1 | 1974-1990 | £20-£25 | $30-$40 | ☐ |
| Lighthouse | 3x1¾ | 1974-1990 | £35-£45 | $50-$70 | ☐ |
| Mermaid | 2½x2¼ | 1974-1990 | £35-£45 | $50-$70 | ☐ |
| Sea Horse | | 1974-1990 | £120-£180 | $180-$275 | ☐ |
| Snail | | 1974-1990 | £50-£80 | $75-$120 | ☐ |

# Characters from Film & Literature

Nothing is more collectable than that which is liable to provoke happy memories from the past. Therefore characters that appear in films, first in the cinema and then on television, are likely to prove most popular, and topping the list are those that have ever-lasting appeal. Here Walt Disney has an unchallenging lead for cinema, and Hanna-Barbera for television characters.

| Name | Size | Production | Market Price | | Acquired |
|------|------|-----------|-------------|--|----------|
| Mickey Mouse | | 1934 | £1200-£1500 | $1775-$2295 | ☐ |
| **Disney (Blow-Ups)** | | | | | |
| Am | $5\frac{1}{2}$ | 1961-1965 | £180-£240 | $265-$365 | ☐ |
| Bambi | | 1961-1965 | £130-£180 | $190-$275 | ☐ |
| Dachie | $5\frac{1}{2}$ | 1961-1965 | £500-£600 | $740-$920 | ☐ |
| Jock | | 1961-1965 | £500-£600 | $740-$920 | ☐ |
| Lady | | 1961-1965 | £175-£250 | $260-$385 | ☐ |
| Scamp | $4\frac{1}{8}$x5 | 1961-1965 | £130-£180 | $190-$275 | ☐ |
| Si | $5\frac{1}{2}$x5 | 1961-1965 | £180-£240 | $265-$365 | ☐ |
| Thumper | $5\frac{1}{2}$ | 1961-1965 | £250-£350 | $370-$535 | ☐ |
| Tramp | | 1961-1965 | £200-£300 | $295-$460 | ☐ |
| Trusty | $5\frac{1}{2}$ | 1961-1965 | £175-£250 | $260-$385 | ☐ |
| **Disneys** | | | | | |
| Big Mama | $1\frac{3}{4}$x$1\frac{3}{4}$ | 1981-1985 | £20-£30 | $30-$45 | ☐ |
| Chief | $1\frac{7}{8}$x1 | 1981-1985 | £20-£25 | $30-$40 | ☐ |
| Copper | $1\frac{5}{8}$x$1\frac{1}{2}$ | 1981-1985 | £20-£25 | $30-$40 | ☐ |
| Peg | $1\frac{1}{2}$x$1\frac{5}{8}$ | 1981-1985 | £20-£25 | $30-$40 | ☐ |
| Tod | $1\frac{3}{4}$x$1\frac{7}{8}$ | 1981-1985 | £40-£60 | $60-$90 | ☐ |
| Tramp | $1\frac{7}{8}$x$1\frac{1}{4}$ | 1981-1985 | £25-£30 | $35-$45 | ☐ |
| Bambi | $1\frac{1}{2}$x$1\frac{3}{8}$ | 1981-1985 | £20-£25 | $30-$40 | ☐ |
| Dachsie | $1\frac{3}{4}$x$1\frac{1}{2}$ | 1981-1985 | £15-£20 | $20-$30 | ☐ |
| Jock (Green Tartan) | $1\frac{1}{2}$x1 | 1981-1985 | £20-£25 | $30-$40 | ☐ |
| Lady | $1\frac{1}{2}$x$1\frac{3}{8}$ | 1981-1985 | £20-£25 | $30-$40 | ☐ |
| Scamp | $1\frac{1}{2}$x$1\frac{1}{2}$ | 1981-1985 | £20-£25 | $30-$40 | ☐ |
| Thumper | $1\frac{7}{8}$x$1\frac{1}{4}$ | 1981-1985 | £20-£25 | $30-$40 | ☐ |
| **Hanna-Barbera Cartoon Characters** | | | | | |
| Huckleberry Hound | $2\frac{3}{8}$x$1\frac{1}{8}$ | 1959-1960 | £80-£120 | $120-$185 | ☐ |
| Mr Jinks | $2\frac{1}{2}$x$1\frac{1}{8}$ | 1959-1960 | £80-£120 | $120-$185 | ☐ |
| Yogi Bear | $2\frac{1}{2}$x$1\frac{1}{8}$ | 1959-1960 | £80-£120 | $120-$185 | ☐ |
| **Hatbox (101 Dalmatians)** | | | | | |
| Lucky | | 1961 | £60-£100 | $90-$155 | ☐ |
| Rolly | $1\frac{7}{8}$x$1\frac{3}{8}$ | 1961 | £60-£100 | $90-$155 | ☐ |
| Sergeant Tibbs | 2x$1\frac{5}{8}$ | 1961 | £50-£80 | $75-$120 | ☐ |
| The Colonel | 2x$1\frac{1}{2}$ | 1961 | £50-£80 | $75-$120 | ☐ |
| **Hatbox (Bambi)** | | | | | |
| Bambi | $1\frac{1}{2}$x$1\frac{3}{8}$ | 1957 | £12-£18 | $20-$30 | ☐ |
| Flower | $1\frac{1}{2}$x$1\frac{3}{4}$ | 1957 | £30-£50 | $45-$75 | ☐ |
| Thumper | $1\frac{7}{8}$x$1\frac{1}{4}$ | 1957 | £25-£35 | $35-$55 | ☐ |
| **Hatbox (Dumbo)** | | | | | |
| Dumbo | $1\frac{3}{8}$x$1\frac{5}{8}$ | 1957 | £35-£45 | $50-$70 | ☐ |
| **Hatbox (Fantasia)** | | | | | |
| Baby Pegasus | $1\frac{3}{4}$x$1\frac{1}{8}$ | 1958 | £40-£60 | $60-$90 | ☐ |
| **Hatbox (Lady and the Tramp)** | | | | | |
| Am | $1\frac{7}{8}$x1 | 1958 | £30-£40 | $45-$60 | ☐ |

| Name | Size | Production | Market Price | | Acquired |
|---|---|---|---|---|---|
| Boris | $2^3/8$x1 | 1960 | £25-£30 | $35-$45 | ☐ |
| Dachie | $1^3/4$x$1^1/2$ | 1958 | £15-£20 | $20-$30 | ☐ |
| Jock | $1^3/4$x$1^5/8$ | 1956 | £15-£20 | $20-$30 | ☐ |
| Lady | $1^1/2$x$1^3/4$ | 1956 | £20-£25 | $30-$40 | ☐ |
| Peg | $1^1/2$x$1^5/8$ | 1957 | £20-£25 | $30-$40 | ☐ |
| Scamp | $1^1/2$x$1^1/2$ | 1957 | £20-£25 | $30-$40 | ☐ |
| Si | $1^7/8$x$1^1/8$ | 1958 | £30-£40 | $45-$60 | ☐ |
| Toughy | 2x$1^1/4$ | 1960 | £120-£180 | $180-$275 | ☐ |
| Tramp | $2^1/8$x$1^7/8$ | 1956 | £25-£30 | $35-$45 | ☐ |
| Trusty | $2^3/8$x$1^3/8$ | 1956 | £25-£30 | $35-$45 | ☐ |
| **Hatbox (Sword in the Stone)** | | | | | |
| Archimedes | | 1962 | £80-£120 | $120-$185 | ☐ |
| Girl Squirrel | | 1962 | £80-£120 | $120-$185 | ☐ |
| Madam Mim | | 1962 | £120-£180 | $180-$275 | ☐ |
| Merlin as a Caterpillar | | 1962 | £150-£200 | $220-$305 | ☐ |
| Merlin as a Hare | $2^1/4$x$1^3/8$ | 1962 | £120-£180 | $180-$275 | ☐ |
| Merlin as a Turtle | | 1962 | £200-£300 | $295-$460 | ☐ |
| **Noddy** | | | | | |
| Big Ears | $2^1/2$x$1^1/2$ | 1958-1960 | £120-£150 | $180-$230 | ☐ |
| Miss Fluffy Cat | $2^1/2$x$1^1/2$ | 1958-1960 | £80-£120 | $120-$185 | ☐ |
| Mr Plod | $2^1/2$x$1^1/2$ | 1958-1960 | £100-£150 | $150-$230 | ☐ |
| Noddy | $2^1/2$x$1^1/2$ | 1958-1960 | £180-£240 | $265-$365 | ☐ |
| **Nursery Favourites** | | | | | |
| Humpty Dumpty | $1^3/8$x$1^3/4$ | 1972-1981 | £20-£25 | $30-$40 | ☐ |
| Jack | $2^7/8$x$1^1/8$ | 1972-1981 | £20-£25 | $30-$40 | ☐ |
| Jill | $2^7/8$x$1^1/8$ | 1972-1981 | £20-£25 | $30-$40 | ☐ |
| Little Jack Horner | $1^7/8$x$1^1/4$ | 1972-1981 | £20-£25 | $30-$40 | ☐ |
| Little Miss Muffet | $2^5/8$x$1^7/8$ | 1972-1981 | £20-£25 | $30-$40 | ☐ |
| Mary Had a Little Lamb | $2^7/8$x$1^3/8$ | 1973-1981 | £18-£25 | $25-$40 | ☐ |
| Old King Cole | $2^1/2$x$1^7/8$ | 1973-1981 | £20-£25 | $30-$40 | ☐ |
| Polly Put the Kettle On | $2^7/8$x$1^1/4$ | 1973-1981 | £25-£30 | $35-$45 | ☐ |
| Tom Tom the Piper's Son | $2^3/4$x2 | 1973-1981 | £20-£25 | $30-$40 | ☐ |
| Wee Willie Winkie | $1^3/4$x$1^1/2$ | 1973-1981 | £18-£25 | $25-$40 | ☐ |
| The Cat and the Fiddle | $2^7/8$x$1^3/8$ | 1974-1981 | £25-£30 | $35-$45 | ☐ |
| Little Boy Blue | $2^7/8$x$1^1/8$ | 1974-1981 | £20-£25 | $30-$40 | ☐ |
| Little Tommy Tucker | 3x$1^1/8$ | 1974-1981 | £20-£25 | $30-$40 | ☐ |
| Mary Mary Quite Contrary | $2^7/8$x$1^1/8$ | 1974-1981 | £30-£35 | $45-$55 | ☐ |
| The Queen of Hearts | $2^7/8$x$1^7/8$ | 1974-1981 | £35-£40 | $50-$60 | ☐ |
| Goosey Goosey Gander | $2^5/8$x$1^1/8$ | 1976-1981 | £80-£120 | $120-$185 | ☐ |
| Little Bo-Beep | $2^7/8$x$1^1/8$ | 1976-1981 | £40-£45 | $60-$70 | ☐ |
| Old Woman Who Lived in a Shoe | $2^1/2$x$2^1/8$ | 1976-1981 | £65-£85 | $95-$130 | ☐ |
| Puss in Boots | $2^7/8$x$1^1/8$ | 1976-1981 | £25-£35 | $35-$55 | ☐ |
| The Three Bears | $2^7/8$x$2^1/4$ | 1976-1981 | £40-£45 | $60-$70 | ☐ |
| **Nursery Rhymes** | | | | | |
| Blynken | $2^1/4$x$1^1/2$ | 1948-1959 | £100-£120 | $150-$185 | ☐ |
| I've a Bear Behind | $2^3/4$x$1^1/2$ | 1948-1959 | £125-£150 | $185-$230 | ☐ |
| Nod | $2^3/4$x$1^1/2$ | 1948-1959 | £100-£120 | $150-$185 | ☐ |
| Wynken | 3x$1^1/2$ | 1948-1959 | £100-£120 | $150-$185 | ☐ |
| Baby Bear | $1^3/4$ | 1948-1959 | £250-£350 | $520-$535 | ☐ |
| Father Bear | $3^1/2$ | 1948-1959 | £300-£400 | $445-$610 | ☐ |

| Name | Size | Production | Market Price | | Acquired |
|------|------|-----------|--------------|---|----------|
| Goldilocks | 4 | 1948-1959 | £300-£400 | $445-$610 | ☐ |
| Mother Bear | $3^3/_4$ | 1948-1959 | £300-£400 | $445-$610 | ☐ |
| Baker | $3^7/_8$ | 1950-1955 | £250-£350 | $370-$535 | ☐ |
| Butcher | $3^1/_4$ | 1950-1955 | £250-£350 | $370-$535 | ☐ |
| Candlestick Maker | 4 | 1950-1955 | £300-£400 | $445-$610 | ☐ |
| Little Jack Horner | $2^1/_2$ | 1950-1955 | £300-£350 | $445-$535 | ☐ |
| Little Miss Muffet | $2^1/_2$ | 1950-1955 | £300-£350 | $445-$535 | ☐ |
| Beggar Man | $2^1/_2$ | 1950-1959 | £100-£150 | $150-$230 | ☐ |
| Poor Man | 3 | 1950-1959 | £100-£150 | $150-$230 | ☐ |
| Rich Man | 3 | 1950-1959 | £100-£150 | $150-$230 | ☐ |
| Sailor | 3 | 1950-1959 | £100-£150 | $150-$230 | ☐ |
| Tailor | $2^1/_2$ | 1950-1959 | £100-£150 | $150-$230 | ☐ |
| Thief | 3 | 1950-1959 | £100-£150 | $150-$230 | ☐ |
| Tinker | $2^1/_2$ | 1950-1959 | £100-£150 | $150-$230 | ☐ |
| **Pluto's Quinpuplets** | | | | | |
| Pluto | $4^1/_2$ | c1937 | £200-£300 | $295-$460 | ☐ |
| **Snow White and the 7 Dwarfs** | | | | | |
| Bashful | $3^1/_4$x$1^1/_2$ | 1981-1986 | £80-£120 | $120-$185 | ☐ |
| Bashful | $3^3/_4$ | 1938 | Rare | | ☐ |
| Doc | 3x$1^3/_4$ | 1981-1986 | £130-£200 | $190-$305 | ☐ |
| Doc | 4 | 1938 | Rare | | ☐ |
| Dopey | $3^1/_4$x$1^3/_4$ | 1981-1986 | £80-£120 | $120-$185 | ☐ |
| Dopey | $3^3/_4$ | 1938 | Rare | | ☐ |
| Grumpy | 3x$1^3/_4$ | 1981-1986 | £80-£120 | $120-$185 | ☐ |
| Grumpy | $3^1/_2$ | 1938 | Rare | | ☐ |
| Happy | $3^1/_4$x$1^1/_2$ | 1981-1986 | £80-£120 | $120-$185 | ☐ |
| Happy | 4 | 1938 | Rare | | ☐ |
| Sleepy | 3x$1^1/_2$ | 1981-1986 | £80-£120 | $120-$185 | ☐ |
| Sleepy | 4 | 1938 | Rare | | ☐ |
| Sneezy | $3^1/_4$x$1^1/_2$ | 1981-1986 | £80-£120 | $120-$185 | ☐ |
| Sneezy | $3^3/_4$ | 1938 | Rare | | ☐ |
| Snow White | $3^3/_4$x$4^3/_4$ | 1981-1986 | £80-£120 | $120-$185 | ☐ |
| Snow White | $6^3/_8$ | 1938 | Rare | | ☐ |
| **TV Pet Series** | | | | | |
| Bengo | $2^3/_8$ | 1959 | £40-£60 | $60-$90 | ☐ |
| Bruno Jnr | $2^1/_2$ | 1961 | £40-£60 | $60-$90 | ☐ |
| Chee-Chee | $2^1/_4$ | 1959 | £35-£45 | $50-$70 | ☐ |
| Droopy Jnr | $2^1/_4$ | 1961 | £50-£80 | $75-$120 | ☐ |
| Fifi | $2^5/_8$ | 1959 | £20-£25 | $30-$40 | ☐ |
| Mitzi | 2 | 1959 | £40-£60 | $60-$90 | ☐ |
| Pepi | $2^1/_8$ | 1959 | £40-£60 | $60-$90 | ☐ |
| Percy | $1^1/_2$ | 1965 | £60-£80 | $90-$120 | ☐ |
| Simon | $2^3/_8$ | 1959 | £30-£40 | $45-$60 | ☐ |
| Whisky | 2 | 1965 | £100-£150 | $150-$230 | ☐ |
| **Tom & Jerry** | | | | | |
| Jerry | $1^7/_8$x$1^1/_8$ | 1973-1979 | £40-£60 | $60-$90 | ☐ |
| Tom | $3^5/_8$x$2^1/_8$ | 1973-1979 | £40-£60 | $60-$90 | ☐ |

# Figurines

Up until the late 1920s, George Wade & Son concentrated on industrial ceramics, but the need to diversify, and with the newly introduced cellulose finishing, it inspired the head designer, Jessie Van Hallen to produce well over 60 different models (some in different sizes as well) of human figurines. These were in production for about a decade, but production ceased when they found that the cellulose was unstable, it turning yellow and then peeled off. The moulds were used later for porcelain figures indicated by *.

| Name | Size | Production | Market Price | | Acquired |
|---|---|---|---|---|---|
| Alice | 5½ | 1927-1937 | £280-£320 | $415-$530 | ☐ |
| Anita | 6¾ | 1927-1937 | £150-£250 | $220-$385 | ☐ |
| Anita* | 6¾ | 1935-1939 | £350-£550 | $520-$910 | ☐ |
| Anna | | 1927-1937 | £400-£600 | $590-$920 | ☐ |
| Anton | 5¾ | 1927-1937 | £180-£200 | $265-$305 | ☐ |
| Anton | 5¾ | 1927-1937 | £250-£600 | $370-$920 | ☐ |
| Argentina | 9½ | 1927-1937 | £350-£550 | $520-$910 | ☐ |
| Babs* | | 1927-1937 | £200-£300 | $295-$460 | ☐ |
| Barbara | 8½ | 1927-1937 | £180-£220 | $265-$335 | ☐ |
| Betty | 5 | 1927-1937 | £80-£120 | $120-$185 | ☐ |
| Betty* | 5 | 1935-1939 | £350-£550 | $520-$840 | ☐ |
| Blossoms | 7¾ | 1927-1937 | £350-£550 | $520-$840 | ☐ |
| Blynken (prototype) | 2⅛ | 1930s | £200-£400 | $295-$610 | ☐ |
| Bride | 7½ | 1927-1937 | £140-£180 | $205-$275 | ☐ |
| Carmen | 9¼ | 1927-1937 | £250-£400 | $370-$610 | ☐ |
| Carnival | 7 | 1927-1937 | £180-£200 | $265-$305 | ☐ |
| Carole | 8½ | 1927-1937 | £250-£400 | $370-$610 | ☐ |
| Cherry | 10 | 1927-1937 | £250-£400 | $370-$610 | ☐ |
| Choir Boy* | 7⅜ | 1935-1939 | £350-£550 | $520-$840 | ☐ |
| Christina | 11 | 1927-1937 | £200-£400 | $295-$610 | ☐ |
| Claude | 7¾ | 1927-1937 | £150-£250 | $220-$385 | ☐ |
| Colarado | 10 | 1927-1937 | £300-£400 | $445-$610 | ☐ |
| Conchita | 8¾ | 1927-1937 | £250-£400 | $370-$610 | ☐ |
| Curls | 6 | 1927-1937 | £180-£200 | $265-$305 | ☐ |
| Curtsey | 5 | 1927-1937 | £80-£100 | $120-$155 | ☐ |
| Curtsey* | 5 | 1935-1939 | £350-£550 | $520-$840 | ☐ |
| Cynthia | 5 | 1927-1937 | £100-£150 | $150-$230 | ☐ |
| Cynthia* | 5 | 1935-1939 | £350-£550 | $520-$840 | ☐ |
| Daisette | 10 | 1927-1937 | £350-£550 | $520-$840 | ☐ |
| Dawn | 8¼ | 1927-1937 | £350-£550 | $520-$840 | ☐ |
| Delight | 3 | 1927-1937 | £180-£220 | $265-$335 | ☐ |
| Dolly Vardon | | 1927-1937 | £350-£550 | $520-$840 | ☐ |
| Elf | 4 | 1927-1937 | £180-£220 | $265-$335 | ☐ |
| Ginger | 9½ | 1927-1937 | £350-£550 | $520-$840 | ☐ |
| Gloria | 5¾ | 1927-1937 | £180-£200 | $265-$305 | ☐ |
| Grace | 9¼ | 1927-1937 | £250-£400 | $370-$610 | ☐ |
| Grace* | 9¼ | 1935-1939 | £350-£550 | $520-$840 | ☐ |
| Greta | 8 | 1927-1937 | £250-£400 | $370-$610 | ☐ |
| HRH Princess Elizabeth | 5¾ | 1927-1937 | £200-£300 | $295-$460 | ☐ |
| Harriet | 8 | 1927-1937 | £150-£180 | $220-$275 | ☐ |
| Helga | 10 | 1927-1937 | £150-£180 | $220-$275 | ☐ |
| Hiawatha | 4 | 1927-1937 | £180-£220 | $265-$335 | ☐ |
| Hille Bobbe | 10 | 1927-1937 | £200-£400 | $295-$610 | ☐ |

| Name | Size | Production | Market Price | | Acquired |
|------|------|-----------|--------------|---|----------|
| Humoresque | 8¼ | 1927-1937 | £150-£180 | $220-$275 | ☐ |
| Jean | 6¾ | 1927-1937 | £180-£200 | $265-$305 | ☐ |
| Jeanette | 6½ | 1927-1937 | £150-£250 | $220-$385 | ☐ |
| José | 4½ | 1927-1937 | £80-£100 | $120-$155 | ☐ |
| José* | 4½ | 1935-1939 | £350-£550 | $520-$840 | ☐ |
| Joy | 9¼ | 1927-1937 | £300-£500 | $445-$765 | ☐ |
| Joy* | 9¼ | 1935-1939 | £250-£400 | $370-$610 | ☐ |
| Joyce | 7¼ | 1927-1937 | £130-£160 | $190-$245 | ☐ |
| Juliette* | 9¼ | 1935-1939 | £400-£600 | $590-$920 | ☐ |
| June | 7 | 1927-1937 | £180-£200 | $265-$305 | ☐ |
| Lotus | 9¾ | 1927-1937 | £150-£200 | $220-$305 | ☐ |
| Madonna with Child | 13½ | 1927-1937 | £400-£600 | $590-$920 | ☐ |
| Madonna with Child* | 13½ | 1935-1939 | £700-£1100 | $1035-$1820 | ☐ |
| Maria Theresa | 8 | 1927-1937 | £200-£250 | $295-$385 | ☐ |
| Mimi | 7¾ | 1927-1937 | £150-£250 | $220-$385 | ☐ |
| Old Nanny | 9 | 1927-1937 | £250-£350 | $370-$535 | ☐ |
| Old Nanny* | 9 | 1935-1939 | £350-£550 | $520-$840 | ☐ |
| Pavlova | 4½ | 1927-1937 | £100-£120 | $150-$185 | ☐ |
| Pavlova | 9¼ | 1927-1937 | £180-£220 | $265-$335 | ☐ |
| Pavlova* | 4½ | 1935-1939 | £350-£550 | $520-$840 | ☐ |
| Peggy | 6¾ | 1927-1937 | £130-£160 | $190-$245 | ☐ |
| Phyllis* | 5¼ | 1927-1937 | £250-£450 | $370-$690 | ☐ |
| Pompadour | 6 | 1927-1937 | £120-£150 | $180-$230 | ☐ |
| Queenie | 4 | 1927-1937 | £100-£150 | $150-$230 | ☐ |
| Queenie* | 3⅝ | 1935-1939 | £350-£550 | $520-$840 | ☐ |
| Rhythm | 9¾ | 1927-1937 | £250-£350 | $370-$535 | ☐ |
| Romance | 6 | 1927-1937 | £60-£90 | $90-$140 | ☐ |
| Romance* | 6½ | 1935-1939 | £400-£600 | $590-$920 | ☐ |
| Sadie | 13½ | 1927-1937 | £250-£400 | $370-$610 | ☐ |
| Springtime | 9 | 1927-1937 | £250-£400 | $370-$610 | ☐ |
| Strawberry Girl | 5¼ | 1927-1937 | £120-£150 | $180-$230 | ☐ |
| Sunshine | 6½ | 1927-1937 | £80-£100 | $120-$155 | ☐ |
| Sunshine* | 6½ | 1935-1939 | £350-£550 | $520-$840 | ☐ |
| Swan Princess* | 8¼ | 1930s | £400-£600 | $590-$920 | ☐ |
| Sylvia | 7½ | 1927-1937 | £150-£180 | $220-$275 | ☐ |
| Tessa | 5 | 1927-1937 | £100-£120 | $150-$185 | ☐ |
| Tony | 4½ | 1927-1937 | £100-£150 | $150-$230 | ☐ |
| Winken (prototype) | 2¾ | 1930s | £200-£400 | $295-$610 | ☐ |
| Zena | 8⅞ | 1927-1937 | £250-£350 | $370-$535 | ☐ |
| Zena | 4 | 1927-1937 | £120-£150 | $180-$230 | ☐ |
| Zena* | 4 | 1935-1939 | £350-£550 | $520-$840 | ☐ |
| Zena* | 8⅞ | 1935-1939 | £450-£650 | $665-$960 | ☐ |
| **British Characters** | | | | | |
| Fishmonger | 3⅛x1 | 1959 | £150-£200 | $220-$305 | ☐ |
| Lawyer | 2⅞x1 | 1959 | £150-£200 | $220-$305 | ☐ |
| Pearly King | 2¾x1 | 1959 | £80-£120 | $120-$185 | ☐ |
| Pearly Queen | 2⅞x1½ | 1959 | £80-£120 | $120-$185 | ☐ |

| Name | Size | Production | Market Price | | Acquired |
|---|---|---|---|---|---|
| **Child Studies** | | | | | |
| *Boy* | | | | | |
| English Costume | | | | | |
| decorated | $4\frac{3}{4}$ | 1962 | £300-£500 | $445-$765 | ☐ |
| Scottish Costume | | | | | |
| decorated | $4\frac{3}{4}$ | 1962 | £300-£500 | $445-$765 | ☐ |
| undecorated | $4\frac{3}{4}$ | 1962 | £300-£500 | $445-$765 | ☐ |
| *Girl* | | | | | |
| Irish Costume | | | | | |
| decorated | $4\frac{1}{2}$ | 1962 | £300-£500 | $445-$765 | ☐ |
| undecorated | $4\frac{1}{2}$ | 1962 | £250-£350 | $370-$535 | ☐ |
| Welsh Costume | | | | | |
| decorated | $5\frac{1}{4}$ | 1962 | £300-£500 | $445-$765 | ☐ |
| **Irish Character Figures** | | | | | |
| Danny Boy | 4 | 1990s | £15-£20 | $20-$30 | ☐ |
| Phil the Fluter | $3\frac{3}{4}$ | 1990s | £30-£40 | $45-$60 | ☐ |
| Kathleen | $3\frac{1}{2}$ | 1990s | £15-£20 | $20-$30 | ☐ |
| Mother McCree | $2\frac{1}{2}$ | 1990s | £10-£15 | $15-$20 | ☐ 225 |
| Paddy McGinty | $3\frac{1}{4}$ | 1990s | £15-£20 | $20-$30 | ☐ |
| Molly Malone | $3\frac{1}{4}$ | 1990s | £25-£35 | $35-$55 | ☐ |
| Eileen Oge | $3\frac{3}{4}$ | 1990s | £15-£20 | $20-$30 | ☐ |
| Paddy Reilly | $3\frac{3}{4}$ | 1990s | £25-£35 | $35-$55 | ☐ |
| Rose of Tralee | 4 | 1990s | £15-£20 | $20-$30 | ☐ |
| **Irish Songs Figures** | | | | | |
| The Bard of Armagh | $5\frac{1}{8}$ | 1962-1986 | £250-£350 | $370-$535 | ☐ |
| Widda Cafferty | $6\frac{1}{4}$ | 1962-1986 | £250-£350 | $370-$535 | ☐ |
| Mother McCree | $8\frac{1}{4}$ | 1962-1986 | £200-£300 | $295-$460 | ☐ |
| Dan Murphy | $8\frac{1}{4}$ | 1962-1986 | £200-£300 | $295-$460 | ☐ |
| Eileen Oge | 8 | 1962-1986 | £200-£300 | $295-$460 | ☐ $3_s$ |
| Baby | $4\frac{1}{4}$ | 1962-1986 | £200-£300 | $295-$460 | ☐ 6 |
| Phil the Fluter | | 1962-1986 | £200-£300 . | $295-$460 | ☐ 0 |
| Little Crooked Paddy | | 1962-1986 | £250-£350 . | $370-$535 | ☐ 0 |
| The Star of County Down | | 1962-1986 | £250-£350 | $370-$535 | ☐ |
| The Irish Emigrant | | 1962-1986 | £200-£300 | $295-$460 | ☐ |
| Molly Malone | | 1962-1986 | £250-£350 | $370-$535 | ☐ |
| Mizky Mulligan | | 1962-1986 | £250-£350 | $370-$535 | ☐ |
| **My Fair Ladies** | | | | | |
| Caroline | $3\frac{7}{8}$ | 1990-1992 | £30-£50 | $45-$75 | ☐ |
| Hannah | $3\frac{3}{4}$ | 1990-1992 | £30-£50 | $45-$75 | ☐ |
| Kate | $3\frac{7}{8}$ | 1990-1992 | £30-£50 | $45-$75 | ☐ |
| Lisa | $3\frac{3}{4}$ | 1990-1992 | £30-£50 | $45-$75 | ☐ |
| Marie | $3\frac{3}{4}$ | 1990-1992 | £30-£50 | $45-$75 | ☐ |
| Rachel | $3\frac{7}{8}$ | 1990-1992 | £30-£50 | $45-$75 | ☐ |
| Rebecca | $3\frac{7}{8}$ | 1990-1992 | £30-£50 | $45-$75 | ☐ |
| Sarah | $3\frac{3}{4}$ | 1990-1992 | £30-£50 | $45-$75 | ☐ |
| Amanda | 4 | 1991-1992 | £30-£50 | $45-$75 | ☐ |
| Anita | $3\frac{3}{4}$ | 1991-1992 | £30-£50 | $45-$75 | ☐ |
| Belinda | $3\frac{3}{4}$ | 1991-1992 | £30-£50 | $45-$75 | ☐ |
| Diane | $3\frac{3}{4}$ | 1991-1992 | £30-£50 | $45-$75 | ☐ |
| Emma | 4 | 1991-1992 | £30-£50 | $45-$75 | ☐ |
| Lucy | $3\frac{3}{4}$ | 1991-1992 | £30-£50 | $45-$75 | ☐ |

| Name | Size | Production | Market Price | | Acquired |
|---|---|---|---|---|---|
| Melissa | 4 | 1991-1992 | £30-£50 | $45-$75 | ☐ |
| Natalie | 4 | 1991-1992 | £30-£50 | $45-$75 | ☐ |
| **Pageant** | | | | | |
| King Henry VIII (cellulose) | 4½ | 1927-1937 | £500-£800 | $740-$1225 | ☐ |
| Queen Elizabeth (cellulose) | 4³/₈ | | £500-£800 | $740-$1225 | ☐ |
| *(There are six other figurines in this group)* | | | | | |
| Knight Templar | 9⁵/₈ | 1991 | £200-£300 | $295-$460 | ☐ |
| **Sophisticated Ladies** | | | | | |
| Emily | 5³/₄ | 1991-1992 | £70-£90 | $105-$140 | ☐ |
| Felicity | 6 | 1991-1992 | £70-£90 | $105-$140 | ☐ |
| Roxanne | 5³/₄ | 1991-1992 | £70-£90 | $105-$140 | ☐ |
| Susannah | 6 | 1991-1992 | £70-£90 | $105-$140 | ☐ |

# Mabel Lucie Attwell

Mabel Lucie Attwell was a popular illustrator, who created young children who had chubby rosy cheeks, blue eyes, plump stomachs and stubby legs. Her work appeared in countless magazines, books and postcards during the late 1950s and early 1960s. The set comprises a boy and a girl, both walking a dog on a lead and were designed by Paul Zalman. The original cost of the figures was six shillings and eleven pence (£0.35/$0.70).

| Name | Size | Production | Market Price | | Acquired |
|---|---|---|---|---|---|
| Sam | 3⅛x3 | 1959 | £150-£200 | $220-$305 | ☐ |
| Sarah | 3x4 | 1959 | £150-£200 | $220-$305 | ☐ |

# Miscellaneous

| Name | Size | Production | Market Price | | Acquired |
|---|---|---|---|---|---|
| Bisto Kids condiment set | 4 | mid 1970s | £125-£150 | $185-$230 | ☐ |
| *Zoo Lights* | | | | | |
| Camel | 1³/₄x1³/₄ | 1959 | £10-£20 | $15-$30 | ☐ |
| Husky | 1³/₄x1³/₄ | 1959 | £10-£20 | $15-$30 | ☐ |
| West Highland Terrier | 1³/₄x1³/₄ | 1959 | £10-£20 | $15-$30 | ☐ |
| Baby Polar Bear | 1³/₄x1³/₄ | 1959 | £10-£20 | $15-$30 | ☐ |
| Baby Polar Bear | 1³/₄x1³/₄ | 1959 | £10-£20 | $15-$30 | ☐ |
| Corgi | 1³/₄x1³/₄ | 1959 | £10-£20 | $15-$30 | ☐ |
| Hare | 1³/₄x1³/₄ | 1959 | £10-£20 | $15-$30 | ☐ |
| Llama | 1³/₄x1³/₄ | 1959 | £10-£20 | $15-$30 | ☐ |
| Boxer | 1³/₄x1³/₄ | 1959 | £10-£20 | $15-$30 | ☐ |
| Snowy Owl | 1³/₄x1³/₄ | 1959 | £10-£20 | $15-$30 | ☐ |

# Premium & Promotion

Probably the most common way that anyone starts a collection. Receiving a free gift with any product has always been a popular gimmick with manufacturers, especially if it is of popular appeal and fairly high quality, that you will want to acquire the set. George Wade & Son Ltd decided in the mid 1960s to enter this up and coming lucrative market, and began with about 20 different models. By 1968 this had increased to well over 40, and it was from this that Red Rose Tea made by Brooke Bond Foods of Canada, chose 32 to form a promotion. This proved so successful, that Wade added another 28 figures and sold them retail under the trade name of Whimsies. Of the original 32 models, seven were never included in the retail range, (Frog – same mould as Bull Frog Whimsie but was coloured green/yellow – Butterfly, Poodle, Seal, Angel Fish, Terrapin and Alligator).

| Name | Size | Production | Market Price | | Acquired |
|---|---|---|---|---|---|
| **Miscellaneous** | | | | | |
| Black Zebra | $1\frac{5}{8}$x$1\frac{3}{8}$ | mid 1960s | £15-£20 | $20-$30 | ☐ |
| Brown Bear | $1\frac{5}{8}$x1 | mid 1960s | £10-£20 | $15-$30 | ☐ |
| **Balding & Mansell** | | | | | |
| Bronti | 1x$1\frac{1}{2}$ | 1965 | £12-£18 | $20-$25 | ☐ |
| Dino | $1\frac{3}{8}$x$1\frac{3}{8}$ | 1965 | £12-£18 | $20-$25 | ☐ |
| Rhino | 1x$1\frac{5}{8}$ | 1965 | £12-£18 | $20-$25 | ☐ |
| Tiger | $1\frac{1}{2}$x1 | 1965 | £12-£18 | $20-$25 | ☐ |
| **Pos-ner Associates Sherwood Forest** | | | | | |
| Friar Tuck | $1\frac{3}{4}$ | 1989-1990 | £20-£25 | $30-$40 | ☐ |
| Maid Marian | $2\frac{5}{8}$ | 1989-1990 | £20-£25 | $30-$40 | ☐ |
| Robin Hood | $2\frac{3}{4}$ | 1989-1990 | £20-£25 | $30-$40 | ☐ |
| **Red Rose Tea** | | | | | |
| Old King Cole | $1\frac{1}{2}$x1 | 1971-1979 | £8-£12 | $10-$20 | ☐ |
| Little Jack Horner | $1\frac{3}{8}$x1 | 1971-1979 | £5-£10 | $7-$15 | ☐ |
| Humpty Dumpty | $1\frac{1}{2}$x$\frac{7}{8}$ | 1971-1979 | £5-£10 | $7-$15 | ☐ |
| Jack | $1\frac{1}{4}$x$1\frac{1}{4}$ | 1971-1979 | £8-£12 | $10-$20 | ☐ |
| Jill | $1\frac{1}{8}$x$1\frac{1}{4}$ | 1971-1979 | £8-£12 | $10-$20 | ☐ |
| Tom the Piper's Son | $1\frac{5}{8}$x$1\frac{3}{8}$ | 1971-1979 | £8-£12 | $10-$20 | ☐ |
| Little Boy Blue | $1\frac{5}{8}$x1 | 1971-1979 | £8-£12 | $10-$20 | ☐ |
| Little Miss Muffet | $1\frac{1}{2}$x$1\frac{3}{8}$ | 1971-1979 | £5-£10 | $7-$15 | ☐ |
| Pied Piper | $1\frac{3}{4}$x$1\frac{1}{8}$ | 1971-1979 | £8-£12 | $10-$20 | ☐ |
| Doctor Foster | $1\frac{3}{4}$x$\frac{7}{8}$ | 1971-1979 | £8-£12 | $10-$20 | ☐ |
| Mother Goose | $1\frac{5}{8}$x$1\frac{1}{4}$ | 1971-1979 | £10-£15 | $15-$20 | ☐ |
| Old Woman Who Lived Lived in a Shoe | $1\frac{3}{8}$x$1\frac{5}{8}$ | 1971-1979 | £8-£12 | $10-$20 | ☐ |
| Goosey Gander | $1\frac{3}{8}$x1 | 1971-1979 | £5-£10 | $7-$15 | ☐ |
| Wee Willie Winkie | $1\frac{3}{4}$x1 | 1971-1979 | £5-£10 | $7-$15 | ☐ |
| Little Bo Peep | $1\frac{3}{4}$x$\frac{3}{4}$ | 1971-1979 | £5-£10 | $7-$15 | ☐ |
| Three Bears | $1\frac{3}{8}$x$1\frac{1}{2}$ | 1971-1979 | £18-£25 | $25-$40 | ☐ |
| Puss In Boots | $1\frac{3}{4}$x$\frac{3}{4}$ | 1971-1979 | £18-£25 | $25-$40 | ☐ |
| The House That Jack Built | $1\frac{1}{4}$x$1\frac{1}{4}$ | 1971-1979 | £10-£15 | $15-$20 | ☐ |
| Little Red Riding Hood | $1\frac{3}{4}$x$\frac{7}{8}$ | 1971-1979 | £5-£10 | $7-$15 | ☐ |
| Queen of Hearts | | | | | |
|   – Two large hearts | $1\frac{3}{4}$x1 | 1971-1979 | £10-£20 | $15-$30 | ☐ |
|   – Two small hearts | $1\frac{3}{4}$x1 | 1971-1979 | £10-£20 | $15-$30 | ☐ |
|   – Multi-hearts | $1\frac{3}{4}$x1 | 1971-1979 | £10-£20 | $15-$30 | ☐ |
| Baa Baa Black Sheep | $\frac{7}{8}$x$1\frac{1}{8}$ | 1971-1979 | £10-£15 | $15-$20 | ☐ |

| Name | Size | Production | Market Price | | Acquired |
|------|------|-----------|--------------|--------|--------|
| Hickory Dickory Dock | $1^3/_4$x$^3/_4$ | 1971-1979 | £5-£10 | $7-$15 | ☐ |
| Gingerbread Man | $1^5/_8$x$1^1/_{16}$ | 1971-1979 | £30-£40 | $45-$60 | ☐ |
| Cat and the Fiddle | $1^7/_8$x1 | 1971-1979 | £15-£20 | $20-$30 | ☐ |
| Frog | $^7/_8$x$^1/_8$ | 1967-1973 | £8-£12 | $10-$20 | ☐ |
| Butterfly | $^1/_2$x$1^3/_4$ | 1967-1973 | £8-£12 | $10-$20 | ☐ |
| Poodle | $1^5/_8$x$1^5/_8$ | 1967-1973 | £5-£10 | $7-$15 | ☐ |
| Seal | $1^1/_2$x$1^1/_4$ | 1967-1973 | £8-£12 | $10-$20 | ☐ |
| Angel Fish | $1^1/_4$x$1^3/_8$ | 1967-1973 | £8-£12 | $10-$20 | ☐ |
| Terrapin | $^3/_8$x$1^5/_8$ | 1967-1973 | £8-£12 | $10-$20 | ☐ |
| Alligator | $^1/_2$x$1^1/_2$ | 1967-1973 | £8-£12 | $10-$20 | ☐ |
| **Robertsons Gollies** | | | | | |
| Accordian Player | $2^5/_8$ | 1960s | £150-£200 | $220-$305 | ☐ |
| Clarinet Player | $2^5/_8$ | 1960s | £150-£200 | $220-$305 | ☐ |
| Double Bass Player | $2^5/_8$ | 1960s | £150-£200 | $220-$305 | ☐ |
| Saxophone Player | $2^5/_8$ | 1960s | £150-£200 | $220-$305 | ☐ |
| Trumpet Player | $2^5/_8$ | 1960s | £150-£200 | $220-$305 | ☐ |
| **Slimbridge Wildfowl Trust** | | | | | |
| Ruddy Duck (ltd ed 3400) | $1^3/_8$ | 1976 | £150-£200 | $220-$305 | ☐ |

# Snippets

*Set 1*

| Name | Size | Production | Market Price | | Acquired |
|------|------|-----------|--------------|--------|--------|
| The Mayflower | $2^1/_4$x$1^1/_2$ | 1956-1958 | £50-£80 | $75-$120 | ☐ |
| The Revenge | $2^1/_4$x$1^1/_2$ | 1956-1959 | £50-£80 | $75-$120 | ☐ |
| The Santa Maria | $2^1/_4$x$1^1/_2$ | 1956-1959 | £50-£80 | $75-$120 | ☐ |
| *Set 2* | | | | | |
| Bear | $2^1/_4$x$1^1/_2$ | 1956-1959 | £200-£300 | $295-$460 | ☐ |
| Gretel | $2^1/_4$x$1^1/_2$ | 1956-1959 | £100-£150 | $150-$230 | ☐ |
| Hansel | $2^1/_4$x$1^1/_2$ | 1956-1959 | £100-£150 | $150-$230 | ☐ |

# Wade Collectables

| Name | Size | Production | Market Price | | Acquired |
|------|------|-----------|--------------|--------|--------|
| Welcome Home | $3^3/_4$x$4^3/_4$ | 1993-1996 | £25-£35 | $35-$55 | ☐ |
| Togetherness | $3^3/_4$x$4^3/_4$ | 1993-1996 | £25-£35 | $35-$55 | ☐ |
| Fireside Friend | $3^3/_4$x$4^3/_4$ | 1993-1996 | £25-£35 | $35-$55 | ☐ |
| Snow man | 5 | 1994 | £40-£50 | $60-$75 | ☐ |
| Snow woman | $4^7/_8$ | 1995 | £30-£40 | $45-$60 | ☐ |
| Snow children | | 1996 | £20-£30 | $30-$45 | ☐ |

# Wall Masks

| Name | Size | Production | Market Price | | Acquired |
|------|------|-----------|--------------|--------|--------|
| Dyllis | | 1927-1937 | £600-£1000 | $890-$1530 | ☐ |
| Frolic | | 1927-1937 | £600-£1000 | $890-$1530 | ☐ |
| Pan | | 1927-1937 | £600-£1000 | $890-$1530 | ☐ |
| Sonia | | 1927-1937 | £600-£1000 | $890-$1530 | ☐ |

# Whimsie-Land

| Name | Size | Production | Market Price | | Acquired |
|------|------|-----------|--------------|-------|----------|
| **English Wildlife** | | | | | |
| Field Mouse | $1\frac{1}{4}$x$1\frac{1}{2}$ | 1987 | £25-£30 | $35-$45 | ☐ |
| Golden Eagle | $1\frac{3}{8}$x$1\frac{3}{4}$ | 1987 | £25-£30 | $35-$45 | ☐ |
| Otter | $1\frac{1}{2}$x$1\frac{5}{8}$ | 1987 | £20-£25 | $30-$40 | ☐ |
| Partridge | $1\frac{1}{2}$x$1\frac{3}{4}$ | 1987 | £20-£25 | $30-$40 | ☐ |
| Pheasant | $1\frac{1}{4}$x2 | 1987 | £25-£30 | $35-$45 | ☐ |
| **Farmyard** | | | | | |
| Cow | $1\frac{1}{4}$x$1\frac{1}{4}$ | 1985 | £10-£15 | $15-$20 | ☐ |
| Duck | $1\frac{5}{8}$x1 | 1985 | £8-£12 | $10-$20 | ☐ |
| Goat | $1\frac{1}{4}$x$1\frac{1}{8}$ | 1985 | £8-£12 | $10-$20 | ☐ |
| Pig | $1\frac{1}{8}$x$1\frac{1}{8}$ | 1985 | £8-£12 | $10-$20 | ☐ |
| Rooster | 2x$1\frac{1}{8}$ | 1985 | £8-£12 | $10-$20 | ☐ |
| **Hedgerow** | | | | | |
| Badger | 1x$1\frac{3}{8}$ | 1986 | £8-£12 | $10-$20 | ☐ |
| Fox | $1\frac{3}{8}$x$1\frac{1}{4}$ | 1986 | £20-£25 | $30-$40 | ☐ |
| Hedgehog | $\frac{7}{8}$x$1\frac{1}{4}$ | 1986 | £8-£12 | $10-$20 | ☐ |
| Owl | $1\frac{1}{2}$x$\frac{7}{8}$ | 1986 | £8-£12 | $10-$20 | ☐ |
| Squirrel | $1\frac{1}{2}$x$\frac{3}{4}$ | 1986 | £8-£12 | $10-$20 | ☐ |
| **Pets** | | | | | |
| Kitten | 1x$1\frac{5}{8}$ | 1984 | £10-£15 | $15-$20 | ☐ |
| Pony | $1\frac{1}{2}$x$1\frac{1}{2}$ | 1984 | £8-£12 | $10-$20 | ☐ |
| Puppy | $1\frac{3}{8}$x$1\frac{3}{8}$ | 1984 | £8-£12 | $10-$20 | ☐ |
| Rabbit | 2x$\frac{7}{8}$ | 1984 | £8-£12 | $10-$20 | ☐ |
| Retriever | $1\frac{1}{4}$x$1\frac{5}{8}$ | 1984 | £8-£12 | $10-$20 | ☐ |
| **Wildlife** | | | | | |
| Elephant | $1\frac{3}{8}$x$1\frac{3}{8}$ | 1984 | £10-£15 | $15-$20 | ☐ |
| Giraffe | 2x$1\frac{1}{4}$ | 1984 | £10-£15 | $15-$20 | ☐ |
| Lion | $1\frac{1}{4}$x$1\frac{7}{8}$ | 1984 | £10-£15 | $15-$20 | ☐ |
| Panda | $1\frac{3}{8}$x$\frac{7}{8}$ | 1984 | £10-£15 | $15-$20 | ☐ |
| Tiger | $\frac{3}{4}$x$1\frac{3}{4}$ | 1984 | £10-£15 | $15-$20 | ☐ |

# Whimsies

**Series 1**

| Name | Size | Production | Market Price | | Acquired |
|------|------|-----------|--------------|-------|----------|
| *Set 1* | | | | | |
| Horse | $1\frac{1}{2}$x$2\frac{1}{8}$ | 1953 | £20-£30 | $30-$45 | ☐ |
| Leaping Fawn | $1\frac{7}{8}$x$1\frac{1}{2}$ | 1953 | £20-£30 | $30-$45 | ☐ |
| Poodle | $1\frac{1}{2}$x$1\frac{3}{4}$ | 1953 | £25-£35 | $35-$55 | ☐ |
| Spaniel | 1x$1\frac{3}{4}$ | 1953 | £20-£30 | $30-$45 | ☐ |
| Squirrel | $1\frac{1}{4}$x$1\frac{7}{8}$ | 1953 | £20-£30 | $30-$45 | ☐ |
| *Set 2* | | | | | |
| Bull | $1\frac{3}{4}$x$2\frac{1}{8}$ | 1954 | £50-£70 | $75-$105 | ☐ |
| Dachshund | $1\frac{1}{8}$x$1\frac{1}{2}$ | 1954 | £40-£60 | $60-$90 | ☐ |
| Hare | $1\frac{1}{8}$x$1\frac{3}{4}$ | 1954 | £20-£30 | $30-$45 | ☐ |
| Kitten | $1\frac{3}{8}$x$1\frac{3}{4}$ | 1954 | £40-£60 | $60-$90 | ☐ |
| Lamb | $1\frac{7}{8}$x$1\frac{1}{4}$ | 1954 | £25-£30 | $35-$45 | ☐ |
| *Set 3* | | | | | |
| Badger | $1\frac{1}{4}$x2 | 1955 | £20-£30 | $30-$45 | ☐ |
| Fox Cub | $1\frac{3}{8}$x$1\frac{5}{8}$ | 1955 | £30-£50 | $45-$75 | ☐ |

| Name | Size | Production | Market Price | | Acquired |
|---|---|---|---|---|---|
| Retriever | $1\frac{1}{4}$x$1\frac{7}{8}$ | 1955 | £20-£30 | $30-$45 | ☐ |
| Shetland Pony | $1\frac{3}{8}$x2 | 1955 | £20-£30 | $30-$45 | ☐ |
| Stoat | $1\frac{1}{8}$x$1\frac{3}{4}$ | 1955 | £30-£50 | $45-$75 | ☐ |
| *Set 4* | | | | | |
| Baby Elephant | $1\frac{1}{4}$x$1\frac{7}{8}$ | 1955 | £30-£40 | $45-$60 | ☐ |
| Crocodile | $\frac{3}{4}$x$1\frac{5}{8}$ | 1955 | £35-£45 | $50-$70 | ☐ |
| Lion | $1\frac{1}{4}$x$1\frac{5}{8}$ | 1955 | £30-£40 | $45-$60 | ☐ |
| Monkey | $1\frac{7}{8}$x$1\frac{5}{8}$ | 1955 | £20-£30 | $30-$45 | ☐ |
| Rhinoceros | $1\frac{3}{4}$x$2\frac{3}{8}$ | 1955 | £20-£30 | $30-$45 | ☐ |
| *Set 5* | | | | | |
| Beagle | $\frac{3}{4}$x1 | 1956 | £35-£45 | $50-$70 | ☐ |
| Colt | $1\frac{7}{16}$x$1\frac{5}{8}$ | 1956 | £30-£40 | $45-$60 | ☐ |
| Foal | $1\frac{1}{4}$x$1\frac{3}{4}$ | 1956 | £30-£40 | $45-$60 | ☐ |
| Mare | $1\frac{7}{8}$x2 | 1956 | £30-£40 | $45-$60 | ☐ |
| *Set 6* | | | | | |
| Baby Polar Bear | $\frac{7}{8}$x$1\frac{1}{8}$ | 1956 | £25-£30 | $35-$45 | ☐ |
| Baby Seal | $\frac{7}{8}$x$1\frac{1}{8}$ | 1956 | £20-£30 | $30-$45 | ☐ |
| Husky | $1\frac{1}{4}$x$1\frac{1}{8}$ | 1956 | £30-£50 | $45-$75 | ☐ |
| King Penguin | $1\frac{3}{16}$x$\frac{5}{8}$ | 1956 | £30-£50 | $45-$75 | ☐ |
| Polar Bear | $1\frac{3}{4}$x$1\frac{3}{4}$ | 1956 | £25-£30 | $35-$45 | ☐ |
| *Set 7* | | | | | |
| Alsatian | $1\frac{3}{8}$x$1\frac{5}{8}$ | 1957 | £20-£30 | $30-$45 | ☐ |
| Boxer | $1\frac{3}{8}$x$1\frac{1}{2}$ | 1957 | £25-£30 | $35-$45 | ☐ |
| Corgi | 1x$1\frac{1}{4}$ | 1957 | £25-£30 | $35-$45 | ☐ |
| Saint Bernard | $1\frac{1}{2}$x$1\frac{7}{8}$ | 1957 | £30-£40 | $45-$60 | ☐ |
| West Highland Terrier | 1x$1\frac{1}{4}$ | 1957 | £25-£30 | $35-$45 | ☐ |
| *Set 8* | | | | | |
| Bactrian Camel | $1\frac{1}{2}$x$1\frac{5}{8}$ | 1958 | £20-£30 | $30-$45 | ☐ |
| Cockatoo | $1\frac{1}{8}$x$1\frac{1}{4}$ | 1958 | £25-£30 | $35-$45 | ☐ |
| Giant Panda | $1\frac{1}{2}$x1 | 1958 | £20-£30 | $30-$45 | ☐ |
| Lion Cub | 1x1 | 1958 | £20-£30 | $30-$45 | ☐ |
| Llama | $1\frac{3}{4}$x$1\frac{1}{8}$ | 1958 | £20-£30 | $30-$45 | ☐ |
| *Set 9* | | | | | |
| Bear Cub | $1\frac{1}{8}$x$1\frac{1}{8}$ | 1958 | £20-£30 | $30-$45 | ☐ |
| Cougar | $\frac{3}{4}$x$1\frac{7}{8}$ | 1958 | £30-£40 | $45-$60 | ☐ |
| Grizzly Bear | $1\frac{7}{8}$x$\frac{7}{8}$ | 1958 | £30-£40 | $45-$60 | ☐ |
| Racoon | $1\frac{1}{8}$x$1\frac{1}{8}$ | 1958 | £20-£30 | $30-$45 | ☐ |
| Snowy Owl | $1\frac{1}{8}$x$1\frac{3}{16}$ | 1958 | £30-£40 | $45-$60 | ☐ |
| *Set 10* | | | | | |
| Foxhound | 1x$1\frac{3}{4}$ | 1959 | £40-£60 | $60-$90 | ☐ |
| Italian Goat | $1\frac{3}{8}$x$1\frac{1}{2}$ | 1959 | £40-£60 | $60-$90 | ☐ |
| Piglet | $\frac{7}{8}$x$1\frac{1}{2}$ | 1959 | £40-£60 | $60-$90 | ☐ |
| Shire Horse | 2x$2\frac{1}{2}$ | 1959 | £130-£150 | $190-$230 | ☐ |
| Shire Horse (brown glaze) | 2x$2\frac{1}{8}$ | 1959 | £130-£180 | $190-$275 | ☐ |
| Swan | $\frac{7}{8}$x$1\frac{1}{2}$ | 1959 | £100-£120 | $150-$185 | ☐ |
| **Series 2** | | | | | |
| *Set 1* | | | | | |
| Fawn | $1\frac{3}{8}$x$1\frac{1}{4}$ | 1971-1984 | £4-£8 | $5-$10 | ☐ |
| Kitten | $1\frac{3}{8}$x$1\frac{3}{8}$ | 1971-1984 | £4-£8 | $5-$10 | ☐ |
| Mongrel | $1\frac{1}{8}$x$1\frac{1}{2}$ | 1971-1984 | £4-£8 | $5-$10 | ☐ |
| Rabbit | $1\frac{1}{8}$x$1\frac{7}{8}$ | 1971-1984 | £4-£8 | $5-$10 | ☐ |

| Name | Size | Production | Market Price | | Acquired |
|------|------|-----------|--------------|---|----------|
| Spaniel | $1^3/_8$x$1^3/_8$ | 1971-1984 | £4-£8 | $5-$10 | ☐ |
| *Set 2* | | | | | |
| Beaver | $1^1/_4$x$1^1/_4$ | 1972-1984 | £4-£8 | $5-$10 | ☐ |
| Bushbaby | $1^1/_4$x$1^1/_8$ | 1972-1984 | £4-£8 | $5-$10 | ☐ |
| Corgi | $1^1/_2$x$1^1/_2$ | 1972-1984 | £4-£8 | $5-$10 | ☐ |
| Duck | $1^1/_4$x$1^1/_2$ | 1972-1984 | £4-£8 | $5-$10 | ☐ |
| Fox | $1^3/_8$x$1^1/_2$ | 1972-1984 | £4-£8 | $5-$10 | ☐ |
| *Set 3* | | | | | |
| Bear Cub | $1^3/_8$x$^7/_8$ | 1972-1984 | £4-£8 | $5-$10 | ☐ |
| Otter | $1^1/_4$x$1^1/_2$ | 1972-1984 | £4-£8 | $5-$10 | ☐ |
| Owl | $1^1/_2$x$^7/_8$ | 1972-1984 | £4-£8 | $5-$10 | ☐ |
| Setter | $1^3/_8$x$1^7/_8$ | 1972-1984 | £4-£8 | $5-$10 | ☐ |
| Trout | $1^1/_8$x$1^3/_8$ | 1972-1984 | £4-£8 | $5-$10 | ☐ |
| *Set 4* | | | | | |
| Chimp | $1^1/_2$x$1^3/_8$ | 1973-1984 | £4-£8 | $5-$10 | ☐ |
| Elephant | $1^3/_8$x$1^3/_4$ | 1973-1984 | £8-£12 | $10-$20 | ☐ |
| Giraffe | $1^1/_2$x$1^1/_2$ | 1973-1984 | £4-£8 | $5-$10 | ☐ |
| Hippo (large) | $1^1/_{16}$x$1^3/_4$ | 1973-1984 | £6-£8 | $5-$10 | ☐ |
| Hippo (small) | $^7/_8$x$1^1/_2$ | 1973-1984 | £4-£8 | $5-$10 | ☐ |
| Lion | $1^3/_8$x$1^3/_4$ | 1973-1984 | £4-£8 | $5-$10 | ☐ |
| *Set 5* | | | | | |
| Alsatian | $1^1/_4$x$1^7/_8$ | 1974-1984 | £4-£8 | $5-$10 | ☐ |
| Field Mouse | $1^1/_2$x$^3/_4$ | 1974-1984 | £4-£8 | $5-$10 | ☐ |
| Hedgehog | $^7/_8$x$1^3/_4$ | 1974-1984 | £4-£8 | $5-$10 | ☐ |
| Pinemarten | $1^3/_8$x$1^1/_2$ | 1974-1984 | £4-£8 | $5-$10 | ☐ |
| Squirrel | $1^3/_8$x$1^3/_8$ | 1974-1984 | £4-£8 | $5-$10 | ☐ |
| *Set 6* | | | | | |
| Collie | $1^1/_4$x$1^3/_8$ | 1975-1984 | £5-£8 | $7-$10 | ☐ |
| Cow | $1^1/_4$x$1^1/_2$ | 1975-1984 | £5-£8 | $7-$10 | ☐ |
| Horse | $1^5/_8$x$1^3/_8$ | 1975-1984 | £5-£8 | $7-$10 | ☐ |
| Lamb | $1^3/_8$x$1^1/_8$ | 1975-1984 | £5-£8 | $7-$10 | ☐ |
| Pig | $^5/_{16}$x$1^1/_2$ | 1975-1984 | £6-£10 | $10-$15 | ☐ |
| *Set 7* | | | | | |
| Camel | $1^3/_8$x$1^5/_8$ | 1976-1984 | £5-£8 | $7-$10 | ☐ |
| Gorilla | $1^1/_2$x$1^1/_4$ | 1976-1984 | £5-£8 | $7-$10 | ☐ |
| Leopard | $^7/_8$x$1^7/_8$ | 1976-1984 | £5-£8 | $7-$10 | ☐ |
| Rhino | $^7/_8$x$1^5/_8$ | 1976-1984 | £5-£8 | $7-$10 | ☐ |
| Zebra | $1^5/_8$x$1^1/_2$ | 1976-1984 | £5-£8 | $7-$10 | ☐ |
| *Set 8* | | | | | |
| Cat | $1^1/_2$x$^7/_8$ | 1977-1984 | £8-£12 | $10-$20 | ☐ |
| Donkey | $1^1/_4$x$1^5/_8$ | 1977-1984 | £8-£12 | $10-$20 | ☐ |
| Mouse | $1^1/_2$x$1$ | 1977-1984 | £8-£12 | $10-$20 | ☐ |
| Owl | $1^1/_2$x$1$ | 1977-1984 | £8-£12 | $10-$20 | ☐ |
| Ram | $1^3/_{16}$x$1^3/_8$ | 1977-1984 | £6-£10 | $10-$15 | ☐ |
| *Set 9* | | | | | |
| Angel Fish | $1^3/_8$x$1^1/_4$ | 1978-1984 | £6-£10 | $10-$15 | ☐ |
| Dolphin | $1^1/_8$x$1^3/_4$ | 1978-1984 | £20-£25 | $30-$40 | ☐ |
| Pelican | $1^3/_4$x$1^3/_8$ | 1978-1984 | £8-£12 | $10-$20 | ☐ |
| Seahorse | $2$x$^3/_4$ | 1978-1984 | £8-£12 | $10-$20 | ☐ |
| Turtle | $^9/_{16}$x$2$ | 1978-1984 | £5-£8 | $7-$10 | ☐ |
| *Set 10* | | | | | |

| Name | Size | Production | Market Price | | Acquired |
|------|------|-----------|--------------|---|----------|
| Kangaroo | $1^5/_8$x$1^1/_8$ | 1979-1984 | £6-£10 | $10-$15 | ☐ |
| Koala Bear | $1^1/_8$x$1^1/_8$ | 1979-1984 | £10-£15 | $15-$20 | ☐ |
| Langur | $1^3/_8$x$1^1/_2$ | 1979-1984 | £5-£8 | $7-$10 | ☐ |
| Orangutan | $1^1/_4$x$1^1/_4$ | 1979-1984 | £5-£8 | $7-$10 | ☐ |
| Tiger | $1^1/_2$x$1^1/_8$ | 1979-1984 | £6-£10 | $10-$15 | ☐ |
| *Set 11* | | | | | |
| Bison | $1^3/_8$x$1^3/_4$ | 1979-1984 | £5-£8 | $7-$10 | ☐ |
| Bluebird | $^5/_8$x$1^1/_2$ | 1979-1984 | £12-£18 | $20-$25 | ☐ |
| Bullfrog | $^7/_8$x1 | 1979-1984 | £5-£8 | $7-$10 | ☐ |
| Raccoon | 1x$1^1/_2$ | 1979-1984 | £5-£8 | $7-$10 | ☐ |
| Wild Boar | $1^1/_8$x$1^5/_8$ | 1979-1984 | £5-£8 | $7-$10 | ☐ |
| *Set 12* | | | | | |
| Husky | $1^7/_{16}$x$1^1/_8$ | 1980-1984 | £10-£15 | $15-$20 | ☐ |
| Penguin | $1^5/_8$x$^3/_4$ | 1980-1984 | £15-£20 | $20-$30 | ☐ |
| Polar Bear | $1^1/_8$x$1^5/_8$ | 1980-1984 | £8-£12 | $10-$20 | ☐ |
| Seal Pup | 1x$1^1/_2$ | 1980-1984 | £8-£12 | $10-$20 | ☐ |
| Walrus | $1^1/_4$x$1^1/_4$ | 1980-1984 | £5-£8 | $7-$10 | ☐ |

# Whoppas

Whoppas were introduced in 1976 and although not exact copies of the Whimsies series, they were larger models on the same theme. The main reason they were introduced was to fill a gap in the product range between the Whimsies and Nursery Favourites.

| Name | Size | Production | Market Price | | Acquired |
|------|------|-----------|--------------|---|----------|
| *Set 1* | | | | | |
| Brown Bear | $1^1/_2$x$1^3/_4$ | 1976-1981 | £8-£12 | $10-$20 | ☐ |
| Elephant | $2^1/_8$x2 | 1976-1981 | £8-£12 | $10-$20 | ☐ |
| Hippo | $1^3/_8$x$2^1/_8$ | 1976-1981 | £8-£12 | $10-$20 | ☐ |
| Polar Bear | $1^1/_2$x$2^1/_8$ | 1976-1981 | £8-£12 | $10-$20 | ☐ |
| Tiger | $1^1/_8$x$2^1/_2$ | 1976-1981 | £8-£12 | $10-$20 | ☐ |
| *Set 2* | | | | | |
| Bison | $1^3/_4$x$2^1/_8$ | 1977-1981 | £12-£18 | $20-$25 | ☐ |
| Bobcat | $1^1/_2$x$1^7/_8$ | 1977-1981 | £12-£18 | $20-$25 | ☐ |
| Chipmunk | $2^1/_8$x1 | 1977-1981 | £12-£18 | $20-$25 | ☐ |
| Racoon | $1^1/_2$x$2^1/_4$ | 1977-1981 | £12-£18 | $20-$25 | ☐ |
| Wolf | $2^1/_4$x$1^3/_4$ | 1977-1981 | £12-£18 | $20-$25 | ☐ |
| *Set 3* | | | | | |
| Badger | $1^1/_2$x$1^7/_8$ | 1978-1981 | £20-£25 | $30-$40 | ☐ |
| Fox | $1^1/_4$x$2^1/_2$ | 1978-1981 | £20-£25 | $30-$40 | ☐ |
| Hedgehog | $1^1/_4$x$1^7/_8$ | 1978-1981 | £20-£25 | $30-$40 | ☐ |
| Otter | $1^1/_4$x2 | 1978-1981 | £20-£25 | $30-$40 | ☐ |
| Stoat | $1^1/_2$x$2^1/_8$ | 1978-1981 | £20-£25 | $30-$40 | ☐ |

# Backstamps and Marks

As with most ceramic firms there are seemingly endless backstamps and types of marks used over the duration of the life of a pottery. What I have included here are the basic types you are most likely to come across. All or most of these will have variations in design. You will also find that there are various methods of making the marks with some marks using several methods, these can vary from the use of transfer prints, handpainting, impressed or stamping the marks into the body, moulded marks and rubber stamped ink marks. In the past ten years there has been a growing demand for personalised special backstamps often designed by the commissioning agents.

## Wade & Co., Union Pottery, Burslem 1887-1927

Backstamp No 1

Backstamp No 2

## George Wade & Son Ltd., Manchester Pottery, Burslem 1922–

Backstamp No 3
1930s. In red and/or
block printed

Backstamp No 4

Backstamp No 5
Late 1940s

Backstamp No 6
1950s-1980s

**Wade Heath & Co., (Ltd.), High Street Works, 1927–**

ENGLAND

Backstamp No 7
1928-Late 1930s

Backstamp No 8
Late 1930s

Backstamp No 9
1940s-1950s

ENGLAND

Backstamp No 10
1940s

ENGLAND

Backstamp No 11
Late 1940s-1950s

Backstamp No 12
1953-1960s

**Wade (Ulster) Ltd., Ulster Pottery, Portadown, Co Armagh, 1953–**

Backstamp No 13
1950s

Backstamp No 14
1954 onwards

Backstamp No 15
1955 with year letter

Backstamp No 16
1970s

Backstamp No 17
Late 1970s

**Wade Ceramics Limited,
1990–today**

ENGLAND

Backstamp No 18

Backstamp No 19

# Faults, Fakes and Imitations

The fact that this chapter is even here is a sign that Wade has reached the dizzy heights of collectability. One could even say respectability, now that a couple of the major London auction rooms have included special sections of Wade and related items amongst the pages of their expensive illustrated catalogues.

Over the years there are certain anomalies that are bound to affect the end product of many production pieces, especially when they are produced in vast quantities. In other words you will always find variations in shape, when the metal die has to be renewed for example or when comparing the first items out of a mould compared to the later ones. In the moulding process itself, when the model is ejected, small bits might get left in the mould. Glaze colouring can also vary, after all humans mix the ingredients, so what can you expect? Once a certain model has been in production for a few months a decision might be made to slightly alter the colouring.

Faults and variations are all very well and often acceptable, once you have satisfied yourself of the problem and feel the price is still fair. What is totally unacceptable is the outright faking of old and even new pieces. The most recent problems seem to surround the model of the Policeman, commissioned by Elaine and Adrian Crumpton in 1993. There are two legitimate versions of this figure, one with a painted face and another with the helmet over the eyes, each produced in numbered limited editions. The fakes would appear to be of the model with the painted face and have a yellow badge and either a pale blue or black uniform. Of the older pieces the Noddy and Big Ears set seem to be on the market in fairly large numbers, the fake models are slightly larger and have been made of a soft body rather than the hard porcelain of the originals. They have also been decorated with bright on-glaze colours instead of slightly more subdued underglaze colours.

The most reported and widely known fakes, made to deliberately deceive collectors, are the Shire Horse and the model of the Swan as seen in set ten of the early Whimsies. Even to the untrained eye the differences are fairly apparent, the fakes having a thicker sugary glaze which alone makes the definition of the models appear crude, but the modelling is crude enough already with a badly defined body, misshapen hoofs and rather a fat head on the horse and a similar lack of detail on the swan. You will find that the Shire Horse even has trouble standing on a hard flat surface. Other such items with similar defects are the Easter Bunny, Bo-Peep and the Kissing Rabbits. The former two are very much reduced in size, while the Kissing Rabbits have features at different angles such as the ears.

In recent years reports have been circulating of other reproductions including: Nurseries, Humpty-Humpty, Little Bo-Peep and Little Red Riding Hood. With these it would appear that the general use of colour is either wrong and/or too bright.

Doubts have also been reported about the reproductions of models such as Dougal, commissioned by Camtrak in 1995, Friar Tuck commissioned by Ian Warner and Mike Posgay and a recent series of Circus Figurines, commissioned by Red Rose Tea for sale in the U.S. only. These models are either being sold far too cheaply, without certificates or in the wrong country. So beware.

In your travels searching for pieces of Wade to add to your collection you will also come across some interesting reproductions. The Studio Szeiler versions of some of the Wade animals. such as Mrs Duck (illustrated in the text), tortoises, etc, are always marked, where possible with the Szeiler mark. These products are the work of the Hungarian immigrant Joseph Szeiler who worked for Wade as a modeller for a number of years before setting up his own studio in Burslem. There are also some direct imitations of Jessie Van Hallen's figures made at the Howard Pottery under the Brentleigh trade name, which are sometimes not marked. Once handled the differences are obvious, being cruder in body and decoration.

This is just another chapter to be added to the story of Wade. It's a sad fact, but true, that having reached this stage you can be sure that Wade products are now officially highly collectable.

# Bibliography

*The Wade Dynasty* D. Lee, Kudos, 1996
*The World of Wade Book 1* I. Warner and M. Posgay, Antique Publications, 1994
*The World of Wade Book 2* I. Warner and M. Posgay, Antique Publications, 1994
*Wade Price Trends, 1st edition* The Glass Press Inc., 1996
*Encyclopedia of British Pottery and Porcelain Marks* G. Godden, Barrie & Jenkins, 1964
*Charlton Standard Catalogue of Wade* Pat Murray Volume 1, Charlton Press, 1996

The magazine of The Official International Wade Collectors Club
*The Sentinel* evening newspaper
*The Antiques Trade Gazette*
*Kelly's Trade Directories*
*The Pottery Gazette & Glass Trades Review*
*The Pottery & Glass Record*
*Cox's Potteries Annual & Yearbook*
*The Antiques Bulletin*